PREACHING
PARABLES

PREACHING PARABLES

A METAPHORICAL INTERFAITH APPROACH

STEVEN J. VORIS

Paulist Press
New York/Mahwah, NJ

Cover and book design by Lynn Else

The views expressed in this work are the author's own and not those of the United States Department of Defense, the United States Navy, or the Navy Chaplain Corps per Section 3-307 of reference (b), cf. *Code of Federal Regulations.*

Library of Congress Cataloging-in-Publication Data

Voris, Steven J.
   Preaching parables : a metaphorical interfaith approach / Steven J. Voris.
      p. cm.
   Includes bibliographical references and index.
   ISBN 0-8091-4506-5 (alk. paper)
   1. Storytelling—Religious aspects. 2. Parables. 3. Spiritual life. I. Title.
   BL628.7.V67 2008
   251—dc22

                                                                    2007047154

Published by Paulist Press
997 Macarthur Boulevard
Mahwah, New Jersey 07430

www.paulistpress.com

Printed and bound in the
United States of America

CONTENTS

To my spouse, Becky, who, as my best friend,
has been my toughest critic and biggest supporter.

Becky, this project could not have been finished
without your love and support.

PREFACE

This project developed out of my curiosity for how parables change lives. For ten years I had used my own parables in preaching and devotional writing with good audience reception. However, I noticed some individuals got the point and others didn't. Messages that should have rebuked sinners were received with joy. They'd remark, "Too bad the people who *really* needed to hear that message weren't here today." I always refrained from replying, "But *you* are the one who really needed to hear it!" This project was born from my curiosity about why some hearers didn't always "get" the parable. The material on hypocrisy came first, and further curiosity for how parables are structured and crafted started my search for a comprehensive guide to parables. When I couldn't find one, I explored the subject on my own and this book resulted.

As a genre of literature, parables are neglected. Parables are more than short stories, less than sermons, too convoluted to be riddles, and more substantive than simple metaphors. While there is a plethora of works interpreting Jesus's parables, little academic work has been done on parables as a separate genre of literature. Seven characteristics that set parables apart from other genres of literature are outlined in this book.

For centuries, parables have been enjoyed without a full understanding of how they worked in the minds of hearers. Parables have resisted being pigeonholed. The dissecting done in this book will add to understanding without robbing parables of their power. I hope the general reader will find it useful, along with religious professionals and readers interested in transformation. May the parables continue to affect readers with great power.

Parables are not unique to Christianity. They have been used in literature and religion to change lives from ancient times.

Examples of parables can be found in the teachings of all major religions: Judaism, Buddhism, Christianity, Islam, as well as many indigenous Native American and African religions. Hebrew prophets used parables to make cutting points, and Jewish rabbis have frequently used parables to elucidate the meaning of Torah. Buddha used parables, and hundreds of parables exist in Buddhist traditions. The Sufi masters of Islam have become experts in the parabolic art and have felt free to adapt older parables for use with modern audiences. Though there are a handful of Christian ministers who have crafted their own parables for teaching through the centuries, they are the exception. The Christian tradition has generally deferred to Jesus and used his parables in preaching and teaching.

Adolph Jülicher is credited with starting the twentieth-century paradigm shift that moved the interpretation of Jesus's parables away from the allegorical approach to a historical-critical approach. Jülicher stated each one of Jesus's parables has one primary meaning, and twentieth-century parable scholars spent their energy searching for the original meaning of each parable. The correct way of preaching parables became explaining what Jesus originally intended and translating that message into a twentieth-century moral. Unfortunately, scholars couldn't agree on the original meaning Jesus intended, and Christian audiences have tired of parables being robbed of their power through overexplanation. Jokes that have to be explained aren't funny. Parables that have to be explained don't transform.

Within the Christian tradition, much scholarly energy has been expended on interpreting Jesus's parables, but not much has been spent on creating parables for changing people in the present. This humble book seeks to teach leaders how to create modern parables for transformation and use them to inspire change. To that end, we will look at what parables are, how they work, why they are the best way of changing lives in certain circumstances, how context affects a parable's interpretation, how to create parables, and how to effectively use them. Parables are versatile, but for them to have their full impact, the context in which the parable is delivered must be just right. An unaimed rifle does not hit the target, even though the bullet is flawless. Likewise, a perfectly crafted parable will not transform a hearer if it is not presented in the right format. These issues will be discussed in this work, and hopefully readers will risk becoming proficient in the crafting and use of parables in their own lives and ministries. In times of old, parables were used as a common and dynamic teaching tool. They still can be effective today.

Parables are an art form. They are simply words on a page or speech spoken in the air, yet they have the power to transform and change lives. Describing the process of creating parables is much like teaching art. The process requires as much inspiration as it does education. But systematically describing something that is primarily metaphorical is like explaining rainbows with black-and-white pictures. In the end, you, the reader, will have to decide if this effort has been successful.

Albuquerque, NM
November 2006
S.J.V.

ACKNOWLEDGMENTS

Many people helped build my understanding of parables. I've read many books interpreting Jesus's parables over the years, and each has contributed to the process. A special thanks to Dr. Clinton Morrison, who shared one of his own parables with the students of his class on the "Parables of Jesus" in 1985 and gave me the first insight that new parables can be created. Thanks to Dr. William Agnew and Dr. Archie Ryan for giving me encouragement when this project was a mere hope. Thanks to all the church members on whom I've practiced preaching and teaching parables. Your insights on my parabolic attempts were helpful. A special thanks to Louisville Presbyterian Theological Seminary and the Anderson family for awarding me a 2002 Anderson Fellowship for Excellence in Pastoral Ministry. The fellowship provided needed research funds. Thanks to my father-in-law, Rev. Richard Harrison, for helping me track down the last two teaser quotes while I was in the war zone and away from the library. Thanks, also, to Kevin Carrizo di Camillo, my editor at Paulist Press. This book is easier to read because of his suggestions. And, lastly, I want to thank those few diligent souls who campaigned so craftily so I would have the time to work on this project. Even though you meant it for harm, God has used it for good.

All good things coming from this work were inspired by God. All errors, inconsistencies, and confusing language are my own. To God be the glory.

An idea which one comprehends immediately is often not worth comprehending.
                                                            Multatuli[1]

1.

WHAT IS A PARABLE?

Smacked in the Head with a Shovel

A man was in constant emotional turmoil. He was moody and anguished. One day he decided to get to the bottom of his pain, so he took a shovel and began digging up his past. In his backyard he started digging a hole. With passion he dug and dug and dug searching for the past that haunted him. When the hole was eight feet deep, he took a breather. He stuck the shovel in the loose ground above him and sat in the hole with his back propped against the earth wall. He had to dig up his past. He had to find the source of his anguish. Where was it hidden? How could he find it? He would dig down to the center of the earth if that's what it took.

A gust of wind blew above him. The shovel shifted in the soft earth and fell. Smack! The blade of the shovel hit him square on the head. In that moment of semiconsciousness he saw stars, lots of them swirling around an old memory from childhood, a painful memory he had all but forgotten. The stars dissipated but the memory stayed and he experienced the pain of that moment long ago. But in that pain there was also relief and understanding.

As he stood up, he realized that, all along, he had been digging in the wrong spot! To dig up his past he had to dig up those long forgotten and painful memories that had shaped who he was. In that gigantic crater in his backyard he discovered what he was looking for. Getting smacked in the head with the shovel just helped him know where to dig.

1

Getting smacked in the head with a shovel is the way I felt when I had my first transformative experience with a parable. I was driving down the interstate thinking about Jesus's parable of the mustard seed:

> The kingdom of heaven is like a mustard seed that someone took and sowed in his field; it is the smallest of all the seeds, but when it has grown it is the greatest of shrubs and becomes a tree, so that the birds of the air come and make nests in its branches. (Matt 13:31–32)

I had heard the parable in church before. I had read it myself several times. I could even have explained the meaning of the parable to others. But that moment, driving down the interstate, was the first time the meaning of the parable became real to me. I could be the mustard bush that gave refuge to the birds! The seed of faith planted in my heart during childhood had finally grown up to be a tree. The insight was profound enough that I wandered onto the shoulder and almost wrecked the car. Parables are powerful. They have the power to change lives. Getting smacked in the head with a shovel is an apt metaphor for how parables work.

In ancient times, the concept of parable often was not distinguished as a separate genre of literature, but rather was lumped together with other types of wisdom literature, word puzzles, or figurative language. In the Hebrew Bible the word *mashal* was most often used to indicate the occurrence of a parable. *Mashal* was an all-encompassing term. Having cataloged all the occurrences of *mashal* in the Hebrew Bible, George Landes observed that the context of each usage of *mashal* indicated one of five different definitions:

1. A proverb,
2. A satirical taunt song,
3. A prophetic oracle,

4. A didactic poem, or
5. The allegorizing parable.

The common spirit of intention that linked each of the *mashal* usages was that each provided a moral lesson to hearers.[2] The *mashal,* or parable, was a teaching tool. Later, in post-biblical Judaism, the definition of *mashal* was broadened to mean figurative forms of speech of every kind: parable, similitude, allegory, fable, proverb, apocalyptic revelation, riddle, symbol, pseudonym, fictitious person, example, theme, argument, apology, refutation, or jest.[3]

Our English word *parable* is simply the transliteration of the Greek word *parabola. Parabola* is the Greek compound word consisting of the prefix *para* meaning "beside" and the verb *ballein* meaning "to throw." *Parabola* literally means "to throw beside," and in Greek usage nominally means "comparison" or "to place side by side." In the New Testament, *parabola* was used with a correspondingly broad sense of meaning as was the word *mashal* in the Hebrew Bible. In English, a specific set of new words has been coined to further clarify a writer's intended meaning when he or she enters the realm of figurative language. More specific English words like *riddle, proverb, parable, fable, similitude,* and *pun* have replaced the broader concepts of *mashal* in Hebrew and *parabola* in Greek. In English, the word *parable* is more restricted in meaning than its antecedent terms in Hebrew and Greek, and it points toward a specific genre of figurative literature that is complex and difficult to define in a simple way. Here are a few typical attempts:

> Parable: a usually short fictitious story that illustrates a moral attitude or a religious principle. *(Webster's New Collegiate Dictionary)*[4]

> The old definition, "an earthly story with a heavenly meaning," can hardly be improved. (George Buttrick)[5]

> In a parable, we lay one life situation alongside of another completely different kind of life situation, and illustrate the one by the other. (Clarence Edward Macartney)[6]

A parable is a brief tale of real things and persons, carrying along with it (or beside it) a deeper meaning. It suggests a hidden picture to the mind's eye. It whispers a message to the inward ear. (Henry Van Dyke)[7]

At its simplest the parable is a metaphor or simile drawn from nature or common life, arresting the hearer by its vividness or strangeness, and leaving the mind in sufficient doubt about its precise application to tease it into active thought. (C. H. Dodd)[8]

The parable is a "language event" in which the hearer is drawn into the parable because it is metaphorical and puts together two fundamentally unlike referents that force the imagination to draw connections. (Robert Funk)[9]

Parables are "paradox formed into narrative." (Corbins Carnell and Madeleine Boucher)[10]

Each of these definitions has its merit and sheds insight on the literary concept of parable. Parables are complicated. They are not easily confined to a chain of defining words. But parables do have a set of characteristics that differentiate them from other forms of literature. Without question, parables share common characteristics with other genres of literature, but they still have enough uniqueness to form their own separate genre. As with all forms of literature, there are always exceptions to every rule; some parables may not fit every characteristic exactly like every other. Rules in literature are not intended for restricting usage to a particularly narrow type, but for helping students categorize and learn how literature works. Every literary rule has notable exceptions. The same is true for parables. For teaching purposes, let us make a list of characteristics that most (but maybe not all) parables have in common.

Parables, as a genre of literature, are distinguished by seven characteristics:

1. Parables are primarily narrative stories;
2. Parables deal in the realm of metaphor;

3. Parables are brief;
4. Parables have a teaching or transformative intention;
5. Parables have unexpected twists that give the hearers pause for thought;
6. The interpretations of parables are context sensitive; and
7. Parables act on hearers covertly.

Let's look at these characteristics in more detail.

First, parables are primarily narrative stories. The plot, characterization, dialogue, viewpoint, and other literary devices used to shape any short story can be effectively used in parables. Andrew M. Greeley wrote, "Every child, and the child in every one of us, is ready to plead: Tell me a story. For the role of stories is to explain life, and the good stories, in their very substance and in the structure of their language, become revelation."[11] A parable is a story. A parable differs from a short story not by the type of literary techniques used to craft the story, but by the presence of a hidden message within the story. In, under, and around the narrative story, the parable carries a message designed to teach or transform the hearer. Rarely is that message explicitly stated in propositional form. The story, itself, *is* the message. The story and message are fused together.

The statement, "To find peace, people need to come to terms with their past," is a philosophical proposition. The statement is abstract. This same concept can be communicated in the narrative story of a parable. "Smacked in the Head with a Shovel" presents one such man who is in the process of finding peace by coming to terms with his past. The parable is a concrete example of this philosophical proposition in action; it illustrates the proposition and makes it accessible to hearers on a more imaginative level.

However, the human imagination often works in a variety of equally sensible ways. Precisely because the narrative nature of a parable works imaginatively, more than one valid point can be distilled from a parable. The teller of a parable might have constructed a narrative story with only one moral in mind, but hearers often can find secondary messages that make perfectly good sense. "Smacked in the Head with a Shovel" can also claim as a valid moral the following: "Carelessness with tools can lead to injury." Secondary or unintended meanings can be very valuable, and do not need to be relegated to a lower status. Sometimes a secondary meaning can be just the message a particular hearer needs to make a life change. Hearers must sort through the variety of possible morals presented by the narrative story and must struggle with what the parable means to them. As language events, parables spark the imagination of hearers to seek meaning in the narrative stories in ways that abstract propositions cannot.

Second, parables deal in the realm of metaphor. Sometimes directly describing something does not result in hearers understanding it. In such cases, a more imaginative way of communicating is required. Metaphors are a form of indirect communication that imaginatively use what hearers already know to help them understand something that is unknown or ambiguous. For the most part, metaphors have been a neglected form of communication that have often been relegated to the realm of poetry.

However, in their book *Metaphors We Live By*, George Lakoff and Mark Johnson have shown that most of our language is dependent upon metaphor so that the metaphor actually changes the way people understand concepts. For example, they note that people often use the metaphor "argument is war" when they speak about having a difference of opinion with someone else. In describing arguments, people will use such expressions as:

> Your claims are indefensible.
> He attacked every weak point in my argument.
> His criticisms were right on target.
> If you use that strategy, he'll wipe you out.[12]

Each of these expressions involves the use of a militaristic metaphor such that the disagreement itself is understood as war with all of the connotations this metaphor implies. In their book, Lakoff and Johnson identify a substantial number of metaphorical concepts that have been interwoven into the way people think. Their conclusion is that our language is primarily metaphorical and people should embrace that reality and use it more intentionally. Having a disagreement with someone does not have to be war if individuals will choose a different metaphor for speaking about the disagreement. For Lakoff and Johnson, the essence of metaphor is understanding and experiencing one kind of thing in terms of another.[13]

Some people live in constant pain because they have not healed the emotional wounds from their past. They might not know how to do this or even how to begin. By being drawn into the parable, "Smacked in the Head with a Shovel," hearers get a metaphorical glimpse into the process, and they gain the necessary insight into their own healing processes that enables them to eventually find peace. They experience the process of healing in terms of discovering a treasure in their backyard. By comparing their situation with the man digging, hearers "dig up" their own insight. The process requires hearers to use their imaginations to make that leap, but this is precisely the metaphorical process. Parables primarily act in the realm of metaphor.

While individual elements of a parable can be interpreted metaphorically, the primary metaphor is the entire story itself. This can be seen by dissecting "Smacked in the Head with a Shovel." The hole in the man's backyard can metaphorically represent his search for peace and wholeness. The breather he took can symbolize the frustration of a fruitless search. The wind that knocked over the shovel can illustrate the elusive presence of the divine. However, the entire parable as a unit, in and of itself, is the primary metaphor of concern. In the complex, extended story of the man's process of searching for insight, hearers find a metaphor that can be compared to their own lives. In a parable, the metaphor of the entire story is much more powerful than the small metaphors within it taken individually. Meaning and insight can be found by dissecting a parable, but that also means killing it. Dissecting a parable should be resisted until the primary metaphor of the entire story can be discerned.

Third, parables are ordinarily brief. The extended metaphor of the parable as a whole needs to be short enough so hearers can conceptualize the whole metaphor in a single thought. As the parable becomes longer and more complex, hearers have a more difficult time comparing it to their own life situations. "Smacked in the Head with a Shovel" is able to do its job in a mere 281 words. Still, the parable has a distinct beginning, middle, and end. There is a plot, a plot twist, and a resolution. However, as far as stories go, the parable is minimal. There is no description at all. We don't know what the man looks like, whether he is tall or short, old or young, Caucasian or Native American. We don't know whether his house is in a desert or in the tropics. We don't even know what kinds of emotional wounds have prompted his search. And, in a very compelling way, all of these omissions could easily be added to the story. A novel-length narrative could be written just expanding the outline of the story as it already exists. But adding descriptive details would only distract from the parable's immediate power.

When the parable teller is economical with words in the story, the hearer can be the one who supplies all the description. An Asian man pictures the man in the parable as Asian, and the house as located in a place familiar to him. An African American might do the same. The lack of description in a very short narrative can build hearer identification in a way that a well-described narrative cannot.

A brief parable is also easier for hearers to remember. Long after the parable has been told, hearers can still remember the story because of its brevity. And, remembered later, hearers can continue to contemplate the parable's meaning, seeking to apply it to their own lives.

Additionally, hearers are more likely to sit still for a short story than a long one. We live in a busy world plagued with information overload. Brief parables are more likely to get a hearing in such a complicated world.

Fourth, parables generally have a teaching or transformative purpose even if that purpose is not always made clear to hearers. A storyteller can have a variety of different motives for weaving a tale. Stories can entertain, inspire, terrify, motivate, even coerce. The narrative story of the parable might also serve one of these functions, but the primary purpose of a parable is to teach or transform. Parables educate hearers about something unknown, provide an example to imitate, or seek to provide a transformative moment in which hearers can choose to be different because they compared their life situations with that of the parable and found their current state of affairs wanting. Parables can be a vehicle for transformation.

The parable "Smacked in the Head with a Shovel" seeks to empower hearers to excavate their own pasts and find peace in the present. For those who are able to lay their own life situations beside that of the story, a transformative moment arises in which they have the choice to follow the man's example and dig up their own pasts. In the case of "Smacked in the Head with a Shovel," the author has acknowledged he had a transformative motive in crafting his story. In most parables, however, the luxury of knowing the author's motive is rare, although a safe assumption is that the motive is for teaching or transformation.

Fifth, a parable usually has an unexpected twist that gives hearers pause for thought. The unexpected twist is the hammer that breaks through a hearer's protective walls; it is also the "So what?" of the narrative. A man digs a hole in his backyard. *So what?* Many people dig holes in their backyards. This in and of itself is not interesting. One digs a hole to plant a shrub or a garden, or to level the yard to put in a patio. There has to be a compelling reason for this man's digging up his backyard so hearers care. In "Smacked in the Head with a Shovel," the man is seeking to dig up his past. Hearers immediately see the folly of such an action, but wonder why this man is so stupid. The wheels begin to turn inside each hearer's mind. That he is digging up his past is unexpected! The story has a twist that provokes thought in hearers.

Likewise, a man carelessly gets hit in the head with a shovel. *So what?* Lots of people are careless with tools and get hurt. Why is the story about this man so compelling that hearers should care what happens next? Well, the man is *happy* he got hit in the head! This is the twist. Most people who get hit with a tool are unhappy about the carelessness that led to their injury. The man in this parable savors the injury as a source of insight. In both cases, the twist gives hearers pause for thought.

If the twist in the parable can be foreseen by hearers, then the parable loses its transformative potential. Both comedy and tragedy depend upon hearers taking satisfaction from recognizing a situation and being able to predict what will happen to the subject before the subject knows what will happen. Thus, the man carelessly sticks the shovel in the loose earth above his head without thought that the shovel might fall and hit him. Astute hearers can anticipate the shovel falling. A comedy results if the unsuspecting man reacts as a buffoon. Hearers celebrate that they are not that stupid and take pleasure from the physical humor. Or if the man is seriously hurt, hearers can sympathize in the tragedy of the situation. Both the comic or tragic outcome of the story entertain hearers because they could predict the outcome and take pleasure (or horror) in the ending. That the man found serious insight from being hit on the head with the shovel becomes disturbing to hearers because this scenario could not be predicted. Thus a transformative moment is presented to hearers instead of an entertaining one. Without the unexpected twist, parables lose their power.

Sixth, the interpretations of parables are context sensitive. Each parable has two contexts. The first is the context in which the story is told. As a concrete story, a parable is set in a historical situation. Even though there is a great deal of ambiguity in the context of "Smacked in the Head with a Shovel," there are still contextual elements that ground the story in real life: a house, a backyard, a shovel, a gust of wind, and a man in emotional distress. Other parables specifically rely on knowledge about a story's context to work. Take the example of Jesus's parable of the mustard seed from Matthew 13:31–32. For that parable to work, hearers must have familiarity with the elements in the story. Hearers must know that a mustard seed is a yellow, spherical seed about one millimeter in diameter. The mustard bush that sprouts to life from that seed can grow to eight feet tall. The hearers' familiarity with the smallness of the seed and the largeness of the bush are necessary for the parable to have meaning.

The second context is the life situations in which hearers of the parable live. Hearers will place the parable beside their own historical contexts for comparison. The meaning they draw from it partly depends upon their own contexts. A suicidal woman who was sexually abused as a child is likely to take a different meaning from "Smacked in the Head with a Shovel" than will a well-adjusted, middle-aged man. The level of personal pain being experienced in the present for comparison is part of the context hearers bring to the parable event. Likewise a city dweller who has never paid any attention to growing plants, especially mustard plants, is less likely to be moved by Jesus's parable than a gardener. The two contexts, the one of the parable and the one of the hearers, influence how a parable will be heard and interpreted.

Seventh, parables are designed to act on hearers covertly. Again, this action is accomplished in a twofold way. The intention of the parable's author in telling the parable is often purposefully obscured. And, hearers often receive the parable without realizing that it has been intentionally crafted with their situation in mind, so they are oblivious to the potential impact the parable could have on them.

Parable tellers often have several reasons for obscuring their intentions. For judicial parables to work, the teller's intentions must be kept secret. In dealing with unsympathetic or hostile audiences, the teller's objectives are likewise best hidden. And in certain teaching situations, parables can be more effective if the teller's purpose is obscured.

When dealing with a hostile audience, speaking in parables provides the storyteller with a certain element of plausible deniability concerning the intended meaning of the parable's message. There are no guarantees a particular parable will be successful. While some hearers will embrace the transformative moment it offers with insight and joy, others will simply walk away unchanged. Alas, if all who rejected a message would be so gracious! A few hearers may even be angered that the parable's teller tried to change them. Violence cannot always be ruled out as a possible response. With hearers who are determined to maintain the status quo, the use of a parable to covertly provide a transformative moment is to be preferred over direct communication. With direct communication, there is no way to hide the intention of what is being said. For instance, the straightforward comment, "You need to look into your past and deal with the traumas of your childhood that are causing you to act like such a jerk," might be interpreted as a hostile attack by someone who doesn't want to change any jerk-like behaviors. Clearly, the speaker of such a direct statement is unashamedly asking for change. A true jerk might retaliate.

By speaking indirectly through the parable, the storyteller has plausible deniability as to the parable's true intention. "Why are you so upset? It's only a story," gives the speaker a way out. Even fools who can see through the indirect attempt at changing them are less likely to take offense. Many fools may not even see the transformative moment being offered. The indirect approach of the parable provides a small safeguard if the attempt to change the hearer goes badly.

In the case of hearers, receiving the message hidden within the parable covertly allows the message to penetrate hearers' defenses. A direct effort at communication may be rebuffed, but the parable slips past and works at the subconscious level, allowing resistive hearers to be surprised by the truth and giving them a transformative opportunity to change.

Some parables (teaching-metaphor and example-metaphor) do not require secrecy about the teller's intended purpose. These types of parables tend to be used in formal or informal teaching contexts where the teacher seeks to make a metaphorical point. The teacher can speak directly about her intention as in, "I want to paint a metaphor so you can see how difficult it is to dig up your past." "Smacked in the Head with a Shovel" might follow to give the students a different perspective on dealing with their pasts. The teacher's motives are clear. However, the parable still works covertly within students as the teaching metaphor shapes and molds their understanding of the lesson.

Now that the basic characteristics of the typical parable have been described, let us return to the task of finding a working definition of parables. Taking these seven characteristics into consideration, let's try the following as a working definition: parables become transformative language events when brief, metaphorically shocking stories covertly bring about insight into a difficult subject, covertly provide a model for hearers to imitate, or covertly inspire a change of heart in the hearers because their own life situations, when compared to that of the stories, are found wanting. This definition is not designed to limit what parables can become, but to give students guidance in learning how to identify and construct parables for their own use.

Parables function in one of three different ways. They function as judicial parables, teaching-metaphor parables, or example-metaphor parables. A judicial parable is designed to move hearers to make a life change. The teaching-metaphor parable is designed to help students gain insight into something unfamiliar. The example-metaphor parable provides a model for hearers to imitate. Depending upon where the hearers are in their own lives, the same parable story can function in any of these three ways for three different hearers. But usually a parable's author has one function in mind when the parable is crafted, even though it might be interpreted differently by other hearers in another context. These issues will be discussed further in chapter 3. For now, let's look at why parables are necessary.

It is clear that a parable is really a story event *and not just a story. One can tell oneself stories but not parables. One cannot really do so just as one cannot really beat oneself at chess or fool oneself completely with a riddle one has just invented. It takes two to parable.*   John Dominic Crossan[1]

2.

WHY ARE PARABLES NECESSARY?

Parables in Individual Transformation

There are times when people cannot understand something told them in a straightforward way. Direct speech is not always the best way to make a point. Take the example of a teenaged girl who has a cluttered room. Mom might politely ask her to clean her room, but the teenager may not clean it. Mom might command her to clean her room, but she may intentionally choose disobedience. Mom might threaten to punish her if she does not clean it, but the teenager may stand defiant and accept punishment rather than obey her mother's simple command. She understands completely what is expected; she simply chooses not to be compliant. The straightforward way of communication has not been effective in accomplishing the mother's goal.

Suppose the mother chooses another way of communicating with her daughter. Instead of the direct approach of asking or commanding her daughter to clean her room, suppose she tells her daughter a parable.

The Parable of the Clean Room

Once upon a time there was a young woman who had just moved out of her parents' home and was living in her own place. She had the freedom to do whatever she wanted to do. She didn't have to obey her parents' rules any longer. So, she decided that she wasn't going to clean her house—ever. Dirty dishes piled up in the sink. She walked on her clothes strewn around on the floor. Dust accumulated on everything. Trash was thrown into a corner. After only a short while, the stench became unbearable, and the bugs got into everything.

When she had lived with her parents, she had only been responsible for keeping her bedroom neat. Her mother had washed dishes, dusted, and carried out the trash. Now that she was independent, her mother wasn't around to do those things. She was responsible for all of the cleaning. The young woman hated cleaning and she remained firm in her resolution that she wasn't going to clean anything.

One day a handsome young man knocked on her door with the intention of asking her out to a dance. She invited him in, but he didn't stay very long. He looked around and saw that the young woman was undisciplined and unclean, and he certainly didn't want to be in a relationship with such a girl. So, he politely left and went down the street and asked out the young woman's best friend.

By using the parable, the mother is asking her daughter to think about the larger issue of cleanliness. Teenaged daughters often resent their parents and believe they can live just fine without them. As a way of asserting their desire for independence, they sometimes cultivate a mind-set of disagreeing with their parents even before their parents ask anything of them. It's not that a direct request from parents isn't understood when it's communicated to them. Teenaged daughters are sometimes disinclined to obey. A straightforward request to clean their rooms might not be effective, but a parabolic story might reframe the request in such a way that teenagers might be more cooperative.

Telling parables can inspire change in individuals who refuse the truth due to their own stubbornness or disobedience. Those people, like the teenaged daughter who wouldn't clean her room, often need a different perspective on the situation in order to see they are in the wrong and need to change. Stubborn people need to be coaxed to do what is in their own best interests. To be fair, most stubborn people do intellectually understand that the change will help them. The obese woman knows she would be healthier if she lost weight. The smoker knows cigarettes lead to cancer and an early grave. The businessman, deep down inside, understands that more money can't buy happiness. The Christian knows that daily Bible reading and prayer *do* draw one closer to God. The student knows there is a correlation between studying and making good grades. What a different world it would be if everyone automatically did what they knew to be right! But, they don't. Parables can inspire a change of heart by helping people reframe the presenting challenge so they make safer and healthier choices.

Those whose stubbornness extends to disobeying rules or choosing wickedness are harder to inspire. The Christian businessman having an affair with his secretary has willfully chosen to break the company's rules, God's law, and his marriage vows. The nursing home aide who steals pocket change from Alzheimer patients is willfully being cruel and dishonest. The politician knows accepting bribes is wrong. The slumlord profits by keeping his tenants in substandard housing. The vandal who spray paints racist slogans on a community center intentionally commits a despicable act. Directly confronting evildoers with their failings causes them to be defensive, angry, or sometimes violent. However, when evildoers have the consequences of their actions reframed so they see the situation from a new perspective, there is a greater hope for repentance and change. Parables work wonders for reframing problems, although even after the issue has been reframed, there is no guarantee the wrongdoers will change. Inspiring the willfully disobedient is at best a long shot.

Beyond stubbornness and disobedience, there are people whose self-deception keeps them from perceiving the simple answer to their difficulties. They subconsciously block out the problem and any possible solution to shield themselves from the emotional pain of their situations. A woman who picks up different men in bars five nights a week has trouble understanding why she can't maintain a long-term relationship. The new church youth leader is frustrated when he can't attract middle-school youth to his two-hour Bible study class that consists of him berating the kids on the evils of rap music. The alcoholic says he can quit at any time, but he never does. The hypercritical father doesn't understand why his relationship with his son worsens when he simply is trying to help his son be the best he can be. Self-deception is a subconscious coping mechanism that postpones the pain for another day. Without a true solution, the pain can never be resolved.

Ironically, many self-deceived people can identify their own problem in others and can even prescribe a good solution! But they can't grasp that same solution for themselves. The father waits for the estranged son to apologize first. As she turns on the television and eats a bag of chips, the overweight woman mourns that the twenty-minute exercise program takes too long. The businessman will relax and enjoy his fortune after he closes the next sale. The youth leader believes he will change lives if youth will listen to his moral advice. The smoker convinces herself she will be among the lucky few who won't get lung cancer. The gambler pretends one more roll of the dice will change his luck. After accepting a bribe, the politician soothes his conscience by convincing himself the voters owe him. Even when people *know* what is right, they convince themselves they are the exceptions to the rule. They know the truth and refuse it for themselves, deceiving themselves into believing a lie. Some people would prefer to live with painful problems than do what it takes to fix the problems and live pain free. Such is the human condition. Parables can break through self-deception so true solutions can be embraced.

Some people are not self-deceived but are simply ignorant of the problem and the solution. For those who lack insight into how their actions are personally damaging, parables provide educational moments. The young athlete who rarely showers after practice may wonder why he has trouble getting anyone to be his study partner. The classically trained choir director may not understand why half the choir quit after he chose anthems in Latin. The woman who has lived with abdominal pain for five years may not know this is abnormal. While direct advice in such situations is more expedient, the use of parables can provide the educational moment in a way that preserves the person's dignity. Nobody wants to be told the way they dress or handle personal hygiene issues is unacceptable. Highly trained musicians don't want to hear that their taste in church music is not popular. Nobody ever wants to be told they are ignorant.

The distinctions among whether people are willful in their inappropriate choices, self-deceived, or simply unaware cannot be made by observing their actions alone. These distinctions can only be made by understanding the internal thoughts and intentions of the individuals in question. Asking them directly may not get at the truth. Willfully disobedient people will lie about their motives. Self-deceived people can't answer questions about why they did something because they are subconsciously hiding the truth from themselves. Ignorant people just don't know any better. Observing actions alone leads to wrong conclusions about a person's motives. The athlete with poor hygiene may be sabotaging relationships with anyone who cares about him. The student with poor study habits may need remedial education on how to study. The nurse's aide who takes pocket change from Alzheimer patients may not be calculatingly cruel, but may be a kleptomaniac with deeper psychological problems. Motivations are difficult to discern even if family members or friends think they know a person well. Fortunately, because the use of parables to reframe a given situation works only within the mind of the hearer, the teller of the parable does not need to know whether the hearer has been willfully disobedient, self-deceived, or simply ignorant. The parable works the same in all three situations.

Parables are especially effective when there is a disparity of power between the parable teller and hearer. The mother of the daughter with the messy room is clearly the authority figure in the relationship. Instead of using that authority in a tyrannical fashion to force change, the mother sought to secure cooperation by empowering her daughter to make a choice that was in her daughter's own best interest. Using parables to effect change neutralizes the disparity of power by allowing hearers to choose a healthy option without being coerced. Parables can reframe the presenting problem and elicit cooperation in teacher-student, employer-employee, older generation-younger generation, governing authority-citizen, and religious leader-religious follower relationships as well. They are equally effective when used by the less powerful person in the relationship in regard to the authority figure. Rather than threaten rebellion, the less powerful person seeks to secure cooperation by provoking insight.

Parables in Societal Transformation

Parables can influence groups of people the same way they influence individuals, and they can inspire individual transformations as well as societal ones. Sometimes a group, congregation, or society is stubborn, disobedient, self-deceived, or just plain ignorant of a problem plaguing the community. Prominent deacons who frequent strip clubs might not realize that public ridicule of their activities is damaging their congregation's witness to the community. Despite police efforts to enforce the law, drivers might stubbornly speed through a neighborhood ignoring posted speed limits and creating hazards for pedestrians. Older voters might selfishly vote against a school bond proposal without thinking how that will affect the ability of students to get a good education, which in turn affects the community and ultimately themselves. Even though scientists have warned motorists that air pollution harms respiratory health, motorists still may not explore alternative ways to commute to work. The decision to break a speeding law, vote against a tax hike, take part in immoral sexual activities, or ignore a respected scientist's warnings are individual choices, but the sum of these decisions makes up the society's choice. When a majority makes choices that are hazardous, wicked, or self-defeating, the change needs to happen within the society as a whole. Even a minority can cause such problems that the whole society suffers.

Parables can be used in a group setting to influence individual attitudes. James Earl observed that parables tend to treat groups as if they were individuals.[2] Therefore, a parable designed to inspire a particular group usually has a main character whose actions and attitudes are typical of individuals in the group. The parable teller wants individuals within the group to identify with the subject in the parable story so they are able to lay their own relationship with society alongside the subject's relationship with the group in the parable. If hearers do this, they are more likely to be transformed and change their attitudes, even if those attitudes remain a minority opinion in their own society. Societal transformation is effected one individual at a time, but if enough individuals are changed, the dynamics of the society also changes. When the behavior of a minority creates a larger group problem, the parable can inspire the majority to be more (or less) tolerant. Tolerance for diversity and intolerance for harmful behavior can substantially change group dynamics. Parables are excellent tools for influencing attitudes.

Take the air pollution example as a case in point. Americans have been repeatedly told air pollution causes health and environmental problems. A variety of pollution-reducing solutions have been suggested by scientific and environmental groups. Unfortunately, each solution tends to be more expensive than maintaining current practices, and Americans tend not to invest extra money when they see their neighbors not making healthier choices either. Environmentally friendly cars are more expensive; using public transportation is inconvenient. Smog-suppression equipment increases product costs, making factories that use it less competitive with ones that don't. Directly educating the American public has not significantly changed polluting behaviors. While more education and awareness are needed, most Americans simply won't spend the extra time or money needed to improve air quality.

Suppose a speaker at a church or community gathering told the following parable without mentioning the air pollution issue.

Pebbles in the Well

The village elders were already gathered in the shaman's hut when the engineer stooped through the doorway to deliver his final report. Isolated rural villages were often dependent upon a single water source to supply the needs of the entire community, and this community was having trouble with theirs. The engineer shook his head in disbelief knowing he had traveled 3,000 miles to diagnose a problem that should have been self-evident. He got straight to the point: "Your village's well is nearly stopped up with gravel. I noticed the people drop a pebble in the well every time they draw water. If they were to stop doing that, no further action would be required unless the water table drops. If they don't stop, the well will soon be so clogged that no water can be drawn."

The shaman replied, "Our great ancestor, Ding, dropped a pebble in the well the day he first drew water from this spot and he had good luck all day. The second day he did not drop a pebble in the well and he had bad luck. The god of this place demands a sacrifice. We follow Ding's example and have good luck."

The engineer scoffed, "Soon your village is going to have very bad luck. Fortunately, you have options."

The shaman crossed his arms and said nothing.

The engineer continued, "First, we can dredge the well and pull up all the gravel and debris that is clogging it..."

One of the elders jumped to his feet and interrupted, "No! To remove the sacred stones would bring bad luck. We cannot allow such an abomination."

The engineer shrugged and continued, "Well, your second option would be to dig or drill another well. Naturally, this will be time consuming if you do it by hand, or expensive if you have drilling equipment brought in."

The elders were silent. Finally, the shaman said, "The people will only drink from Ding's well. It is a sacred place."

"Well, I guess there is a third option. Why don't you build a shrine next to the well? Instead of casting good luck pebbles in the well, they can cast them into the shrine."

The elders conferred together for a few minutes in their native language. After reaching a consensus, one of the elders said, "Building a shrine will require time, labor, and money."

The engineer nodded agreement and said, "It's a small price to drink from Ding's well."

The elder continued, "Taxes would increase to undertake a project worthy of our god. The people will be displeased."

"Explain that their children will have no water at all if they do not adapt this good luck custom now."

"Your solutions are too expensive. We are still getting water out of the well, even if it is less. We will continue our old ways. By casting good luck pebbles in the well, our god will provide."

The engineer replied, "Your god will be displeased you have ignored options guaranteeing water to the fourth generation. Save your money now, and your children will drink gravel."

The elder replied, "So be it."

After concluding the parable, the speaker can allow people to discuss the dilemma raised by the parable. When hearers resolve that the village elders are selfish and foolish to their children's demise, the speaker delivers the prophetic conclusion, "As Americans, aren't *you* making identical choices by not buying fuel-efficient cars and taking public transportation to work to reduce air pollution? Aren't *you* hurting your own children by not spending a little more money *now* to keep the air clean in the future?" Having reframed the problem, the speaker helps the group see they, too, are being shortsighted at the expense of their children.

"Pebbles in the Well" is a judicial parable. A judicial parable has four parts:

1. The presenting problem,
2. The parable story,
3. The hearers' condemnation of the protagonists in the story, and,

4. The parable teller's prophetic conclusion, which compares the hearers to the protagonists.

If the judicial parable is effective, individuals might set good examples by announcing to others they will change. Peer pressure can be exerted to convince the unwilling that change is necessary for the sake of their children. If the parable is ineffective, the parable teller might be ridiculed, shunned, or worse.

The Use of Parables in Religious Contexts

Aesop used fables and parables to resolve problems in secular situations. He was an exception. Historically, spiritual leaders have used parables in religious contexts. Surprisingly, most parables told by spiritual leaders didn't have religious themes, but used situations grounded in real life. Most parables weren't religious stories! Religious followers grasped the secular story, and when prompted by their spiritual leaders, they made the metaphorical leap necessary to solve a religious problem. The strange juxtaposition of the secular story with the religious situation often provoked insight.

Jesus's parable of the wheat and tares from Matthew 13:24–30 is typical. The parable is completely secular. A farmer struggles with the nefarious activities of an enemy who sowed weeds in his wheat. Rather than immediately eradicate the weeds, the farmer lets them grow together until the harvest. Jesus compared this secular situation with the kingdom of heaven and let his hearers struggle with the religious applications. Jesus was a religious teacher. His audience was expecting to receive a religious message. By telling a secular story, Jesus caught them off guard and taught a valuable lesson about how religious people should respond to hypocrites.

Preaching and teaching about secular issues can create another set of problems, however. A young priest graduated from seminary and was appointed to a rural parish in Kentucky. On his first Sunday he offended a number of people by preaching on the evils of alcohol. Members of the church council explained to him that a number of parishioners earned their livelihoods by making good Kentucky bourbon and he shouldn't talk about alcohol from the pulpit. The next Sunday he offended a number of people by preaching on the evils of gambling on horse races. Members of the church council took him aside again and explained that several families in the parish raised thoroughbred horses and he better not preach against horse racing again. The third Sunday the priest offended still more parishioners when he preached against the evils of smoking. Members of the church council took him aside again and explained that there were dozens of tobacco farmers in the parish and he better not mention smoking again. Frustrated, the priest threw up his hands and asked, "Well, what can I preach about, then?" Without hesitation an old farmer replied, "Preach against those heathen witch doctors. We don't have any of them among us."

After a few Sundays of receiving criticism over sermons that are too relevant, priests can easily fall into the habit of preaching only about religious issues. A sermon about whether the Roman church was correct in adding the filioque clause to the Nicene Creed in the eleventh century is not likely to create controversy in a twenty-first century congregation. Though that issue provoked a split between the Eastern and Western Church in 1054, modern church members are less likely to become passionate over that sermon than one on air pollution. Clearly, theology should be discussed in the church, but priests and ministers who don't also address secular issues challenging the community do injustice to their roles as religious leaders. The secular and the religious are so intertwined in people as to be inseparable. When religious leaders avoid secular issues involving community justice, safety, and integrity, then a great disservice is done to everyone in the community, secular and religious alike. Tackling these issues can be controversial, but avoiding conflict should not be a religious leader's first consideration when introducing those topics. In religious communities, parables are useful tools for promoting discussion and influencing public perception. "Pebbles in the Well" is a thought-provoking example of how a parable can change attitudes in the church concerning larger community issues. Let's look at why a few historic spiritual leaders and religious traditions have used parables.

Why Jesus Used Parables

Jesus was famous for using parables to inspire spiritual growth in groups. In Matthew 13:10–17, Jesus revealed why he used them to teach people. After Jesus told a particularly difficult parable, Matthew recorded the following exchange,

> Then the disciples came and asked him, "Why do you speak to them in parables?" He answered, "To you it has been given to know the secrets of the kingdom of heaven, but to them it has not been given. For to those who have, more will be given, and they will have an abundance; but from those who have nothing, even what they have will be taken away. The reason I speak to them in parables is that 'seeing they do not perceive, and hearing they do not listen, nor do they understand.' With them indeed is fulfilled the prophecy of Isaiah that says:
> 'You will indeed listen, but never understand, and you will indeed look, but never perceive. For this people's heart has grown dull, and their ears are hard of hearing, and they have shut their eyes; so that they might not look with their eyes, and listen with their ears, and understand with their heart and turn—and I would heal them.'
> But blessed are your eyes, for they see, and your ears, for they hear. Truly I tell you, many prophets and righteous people longed to see what you see, but did not see it, and to hear what you hear, but did not hear it." (Matt 13:10–17)

The key to understanding why Jesus quoted this passage from Isaiah depends upon whether Jesus was speaking literally or figuratively. Unfortunately, or perhaps fortunately, both possibilities make sense. Literally, Jesus could have obscured his message so people would not understand. Figuratively, Jesus was announcing his intention to use Isaiah's preaching methodology.

Understanding Isaiah's methodology requires a thorough knowledge of the whole book. Within Isaiah are two complimentary passages, Isaiah 6:1–10 and 32:1–8, which, taken together, shed insight into why Isaiah used parables within his context. The first passage, Isaiah 6:1–10, tells how Isaiah was called to God's service. Isaiah saw a vision of God sitting on a throne in heaven surrounded by angels. After cleansing Isaiah's lips, the Lord asked, "'Whom shall I send, and who will go for us?' And I [Isaiah] said, 'Here am I; send me!'" Then follows the passage quoted by Jesus. Translated from the original Hebrew instead of the Septuagint translation from which Jesus quoted, the meaning is even a shade harsher.

> And he said, "Go and say to this people: 'Keep listening, but do not comprehend; keep looking, but do not understand.' Make the mind of this people dull, and stop their ears, and shut their eyes, so that they may not look with their eyes, and listen with their ears, and comprehend with their minds, and turn and be healed." (Isa 6:9–10)

The *literal* meaning is God intended for Isaiah to speak obscurely so people wouldn't repent and find spiritual healing.

In the Septuagint version of Isaiah 6:9–10, which Jesus quoted in Matthew 13:14–15, the tense is passive. The Septuagint was an early Greek translation of the Hebrew Bible used extensively by early Christians and by the Roman Catholic Church to this day. The passive tense of the passage indicates God does not intentionally harden people's hearts. Rather, the people's hearts have grown dull and their ears are hard of hearing. They have shut their own eyes. Blame for the people's lack of understanding is shifted from God to the people themselves. God doesn't have to harden their hearts because the people have done it themselves by continual disobedience. But whether the people's hearts are hardened by God or by themselves, the result is the same: the people stand condemned. The literal meaning of both versions indicates God approved that the people be condemned.

The literal meaning of Isaiah's call suggests God lost tolerance for the people's disobedience and was sending Isaiah to preach a convoluted message that wouldn't be understood so God could punish them. If this literal interpretation is chosen, the passage makes perfect sense. Isaiah 1—5 recorded how the people refused to repent when spoken to directly. Since the straightforward approach had not worked, what difference would it make if Isaiah preached in a convoluted way? If God purposefully hid the message so the past sins of the Hebrew people could be punished, that was within God's right to do so. God was not being arbitrary by hardening the hearts of those people because they had been consistently disobedient. God was not being cruel. God was being *just*. The people had many chances to hear the message preached plainly and to change their ways. The natural consequence of being willfully disobedient was punishment. And for those who were wicked and without remorse, the *literal* meaning of the passage applied. However, when this passage is understood figuratively with the whole of first Isaiah in mind, the passage has a deeper parabolic meaning that foreshadows what Jesus meant when he quoted this passage to his disciples.

When seeking to understand Isaiah 6:1–10, a parallel passage provides the necessary corrective showing God was interested in the people's salvation, even the salvation of those who had been consistently disobedient. In Isaiah 32:1–8, a parable was used to describe an idyllic situation exactly the opposite of the historical situation Isaiah was facing.

> See, a king will reign in righteousness, and princes will rule with justice. Each will be like a hiding place from the wind, a covert from the tempest, like streams of water in a dry place, like the shade of a great rock in a weary land. Then the eyes of those who have sight will not be closed, and the ears of those who have hearing will listen. The minds of the rash will have good judgment, and the tongues of stammerers will speak readily and distinctly. A fool will no longer be called noble, nor a villain said to be honorable. For fools speak folly, and their minds plot iniquity: to practice ungodliness, to utter error concerning the LORD, to leave the craving of the hungry unsatisfied,

and to deprive the thirsty of drink. The villainies of villains are evil; they devise wicked devices to ruin the poor with lying words, even when the plea of the needy is right. But those who are noble plan noble things, and by noble things they stand.

This idyllic situation is in stark contrast to the actual historical situation of Judah in the eighth century BCE. Isaiah lived in a corrupt and wicked time. The charges made against the people in Isaiah 5:18–23 describe a situation in which justice had been completely perverted.

Ah, you who drag iniquity along with cords of falsehood, who drag sin along as with cart ropes, who say, "Let him make haste, let him speed his work that we may see it; let the plan of the Holy One of Israel hasten to fulfillment, that we may know it!" Ah, you who call evil good and good evil, who put darkness for light and light for darkness, who put bitter for sweet and sweet for bitter! Ah, you who are wise in your own eyes, and shrewd in your own sight! Ah, you who are heroes in drinking wine and valiant at mixing drink, who acquit the guilty for a bribe, and deprive the innocent of their rights!

In the contrast between the idyllic situation and its opposite is the reason using parables was necessary. The difference between the two situations described in Isaiah 5—6 and Isaiah 32 involves the morality of the culture. In an immoral society, right is wrong and wrong is right. Therefore, immoral people cannot obey direct teachings about righteousness. Comprehending righteousness in their hearts is too hard because they have a perverted cultural orientation toward righteousness. But in a righteous society, right is right and wrong is wrong, so the society is open and able to hear straightforward teachings about love, justice, and righteousness. In a righteous society, parables are unnecessary because people can hear, understand, and obey the first time. In the immoral society, the prophet first has to overcome the cultural bias toward wickedness before true righteousness can be understood. Parables then become the window for reorienting a person's worldview toward a proper God-view of what is just and right.

A further confirmation that God is interested in using varied methods for packaging the message for the people's contextual circumstances is found in another parable from Isaiah.

> Listen, and hear my voice; Pay attention, and hear my speech. Do those who plow for sowing plow continually? Do they continually open and harrow their ground? When they have leveled its surface, do they not scatter dill, sow cummin, and plant wheat in rows and barley in its proper place, and spelt as the border? For they are well instructed; their God teaches them.
>
> Dill is not threshed with a threshing sledge, nor is a cart wheel rolled over cummin; but dill is beaten out with a stick, and cummin with a rod. Grain is crushed for bread, but one does not thresh it forever; one drives the cart wheel and horses over it, but does not pulverize it. This also comes from the LORD of hosts; he is wonderful in counsel, and excellent in wisdom. (Isa 28:23–29)

Just as the farmer uses different farming methods for different crops, God intends that different teaching methods be used with people in varying circumstances so all have the opportunity to find salvation. The farmer properly plants, harvests, and stores each crop to maximize that crop's harvest. So also God desires that each person hear and understand the message of salvation to maximize the number of people harvested.

Isaiah used parables to reorient a wicked generation into accepting righteousness and justice. Parables were used as a teaching method of last resort after more direct teaching and preaching had failed. By quoting Isaiah at this place, Jesus was declaring his intention to imitate Isaiah's methodology. But only those intimately familiar with the whole of Isaiah would understand what Jesus meant. Like Isaiah, Jesus was ministering in an age when corruption was rampant. Religious institutions were full of wickedness. Evil was proclaimed as good and vice versa. Just as Isaiah used parables and indirect teachings to reach his generation, Jesus also resorted to parables to reach his own.

A parable supporting this view is described in Matthew 21:23–32. The chief priests were questioning Jesus on whose authority he was performing miracles. Jesus answered their question with his own question, avoiding the trap set for him. When they refused to answer his question, Jesus told them a parable.

> What do you think? A man had two sons; he went to the first and said, "Son, go and work in the vineyard today." He answered, "I will not"; but later he changed his mind and went. The father went to the second and said the same; and he answered, "I go, sir"; but he did not go. Which of the two did the will of his father? They said, "The first." (Matt 21:28–31a)

Scholars dispute whether the next verbal exchange in the story was originally spoken by Jesus or was an editorial addition by Matthew.

> Jesus said to them, "Truly I tell you, the tax collectors and the prostitutes are going into the kingdom of God ahead of you. For John came to you in the way of righteousness and you did not believe him, but the tax collectors and the prostitutes believed him; and even after you saw it, you did not change your minds and believe him." (Matt 21:31b–32)

If Jesus originally spoke it, he reinforced his point by telling the chief priests they were like the second son while sinners were like the first. If verse 32 was added by Matthew, and Jesus let the parable itself be the answer to their original question, the chief priests had to struggle with the intended meaning and were less likely to take offense even when the gathered crowds understood.

Even though there are four possible responses in the parable, Jesus only addressed two. A son could have said yes and then went immediately. That would have been the ideal righteous response. Jesus didn't address that possibility. A son could have said no and then not gone. That would have been the wicked response. Jesus didn't address that possibility either. Jesus only addressed the two cases where the words and actions were mismatched. The son who said yes and then didn't go would be the hypocritical response. The son who said no and then went would be the repentant sinner response. Jesus trapped the corrupt religious officials of his day into saying that being a repentant sinner was better than being a hypocrite!

Why Buddha Used Parables

Siddhartha Guatama (the historic Buddha) faced a different social context than did Jesus of Nazareth. While Jesus was reforming an existing religion in a time of religious corruption, Buddha was teaching a completely new approach to religious truth in a time when the people were open to new teachings. Teaching in the fifth century BCE around the Ganges River basin in India, Buddha spent the last forty-five years of his life teaching a path to enlightenment. While Buddha certainly met people hostile to his teachings, many people quickly embraced his path. He could be more open about his message. However, he still chose to use parables.

In chapter 16 of the *Lotus Sutra,* it is written,

> Because living beings have different natures, different desires, different actions, and different ways of thinking and making distinctions, and because I want to enable them to put down good roots, I employ a variety of causes and conditions, similes, parables, and phrases and preach different doctrines. This, the Buddha's work, I have never for a moment neglected.

And in another place,

> And the Blessed One thought: "I have taught the truth which is excellent in the beginning, excellent in the middle, and excellent in the end; it is glorious in its spirit and

glorious in its letter. But simple as it is, the people cannot understand it. I must speak to them in their own language. I must adapt my thoughts to their thoughts. They are like unto children, and love to hear tales. Therefore, I will tell them stories to explain the glory of the Dharma. If they cannot grasp the truth in the abstract arguments by which I have reached it, they may nevertheless come to understand it, if it is illustrated in parables.[3]

Because deductive religious teaching was difficult for many in his audience to understand, Buddha intentionally chose to use a guided inductive method of storytelling. Buddha frequently used teaching-metaphor parables and example-metaphor parables in his teaching. Buddha's parables were often introduced with a proverb and concluded with a moral giving the parable an illustrative function meant to clarify his point. Dozens of parables can be traced directly back to Buddha; hundreds of them are found in Buddhist teaching through the centuries. At least five major Buddhist works contain parables as teaching stories.

Why Parables Were Used in Judaism

More than 1,300 parables exist within the midrashic literature of Judaism. These parables are primarily teaching metaphors that illuminate the meaning of Torah. Because understanding the Torah is such an essential aspect of Jewish religious practice, promoting understanding of it is the central task of the rabbi. The early nineteenth-century rabbi Nahman of Bratslav used parables as a communication method of last resort when people did not understand his prayers, homilies, or Torah lessons. The tale (parable) became a garb for clothing the Torah, awakening those who were spiritually asleep. As a teaching method, the tale transmitted the illumination of Torah in a muted fashion that prevented the sleeper from being blinded by the sudden burst of light from above.[4] Likewise, even though rabbinic parables were frequently used in teaching, the parabolic method was not always respected and rabbinic parables have been neglected in modern scholarship.[5]

A typical rabbinic parable consists of four parts: *motivation, hiddush, mashal,* and *nimshal.* The motivation was the troubling Torah passage that was difficult to understand; the *hiddush* was the moral or the principle point the rabbi was seeking to make in the parable that followed. The *mashal* was the parable story itself, and the *nimshal* was the explanation of the parable that shed insight into the Torah passage needing elucidation.[6]

The Use of Parables in Islam

According to Sufi master Ibrahim Khawwas, Islamic teaching method is to "demonstrate the unknown in terms of what is called 'known' by the audience."[7] This dictum is just another way of describing the parabolic method through teaching metaphors. Cultures in which Islam has thrived have been a lot less concerned about systematic, deductive teaching than they have been with teaching through storytelling. Metaphorical preaching and teaching was the primary mode of communicating the faith, and the Sufi tradition of Islam frequently used parables to lay the groundwork for teaching the basic principles of Islam to beginners.[8] Dozens of parables are found in the Qur'ān and hundreds of parables are known within the Sufi tradition of Islam. Parables were freely told and adapted many times for use in each successive generation. Parables were owned by the community and specific authorship of individual parables was unimportant.

In Islam, all teaching is context dependent. Muhammed said, "Speak to everyone in accordance with the degree of his understanding."[9] Storytelling was both popular and effective for mixed audiences containing beginners and spiritual masters. Islam teaches that students are able to hear different things from the same parable or teaching, depending upon their level and development in the faith. Every passage in the Qur'ān is stated to have seven different meanings, each applicable to the level of the hearer's faith. Likewise, parables have multiple shades of meaning for both beginners and masters. Hearing parables repeated is fruitful for serious students, especially as they become more mature and can understand the higher meanings of a story.

The Use of Parables in
Other World Religions and Literature

Cataloging the use of parables and fables in every major and minor world religion is beyond the scope of this work. Suffice it to say that every religious tradition that uses stories to convey religious truth has the potential to use parables, although not every story is a parable. In every culture, the principles outlined in this book will apply for recognizing and using parables. However, each society has its own unique concept of humor, decency, ethics, and what might be understood as an unexpected twist in a story. Readers unfamiliar with a culture might miss a subtle plot twist and categorize a literary work as a story instead of a parable. Some parables that rely on the use or misuse of language to make a plot twist will not translate well. The parable "A Peace of the World" from chapter 4 is an example of a parable that will translate into other languages as a short story that doesn't make sense, because it is designed around the characters' misunderstanding of the homonyms *peace* and *piece*.

Parables are also found in literature with no apparent religious motives. Franz Kafka was a master of the parabolic art. I am indebted to him for helping me identify several of the parabolic literary styles described in chapter 4. A list of other authors from around the world who have written literary parables is found in the annotated bibliography at the end of this book.

*Allah is the Light of the heavens and the earth. The parable of His
Light is as if there were a Niche and within it a Lamp: The Lamp
enclosed in Glass; the glass as it were a brilliant star: Lit from a
blessed Tree, an Olive, neither of the East nor of the West, whose Oil
is well-nigh luminous, though fire scarce touched it: Light upon
Light! Allah doth guide whom He will to His light: Allah doth set
forth Parables for men: and Allah doth know all things.*

Qur'ān 24:35

3.

HOW DO PARABLES WORK?

Parables function in one of three basic ways. A *judicial* parable
moves hearers to make a life change. The *teaching-metaphor* parable helps students gain insight into something unfamiliar. The
example-metaphor parable provides a model for hearers to imitate.
Again, the classification of parables by type is for teaching purposes. Hearers of the parable do not have to understand a parable's
type or even how the parable functions in order to gain insight and
benefit from hearing it. Understanding the subtleties of how parables work allows the teller to craft parables with specific situations
in mind to increase the probability that it will function as planned.
Let's look more closely at the three ways parables function.

Judicial Parables

There was a man who had lots of problems. He was overweight
and he drank too much. He was estranged from his teenaged children and his wife would hardly speak to him, let alone do other
things with him. He was in a dead-end job and his only hobby con-

sisted of watching reruns of long-canceled television programs. His life was pathetic. When he started to tell a friend about his problems, his friend cut him off and told him a story instead.

The Parable of the Broken Computer

There was a man who had a computer. He used it continuously. Constantly, night and day he ran programs and surfed the Internet and used that computer to its capacity. It was never turned off. Over time, the computer started to have glitches that interrupted the man's work. He started losing data and the printer refused to cooperate. For months and months the man tolerated these problems. One day he got a brilliant idea: He installed an antivirus program that removed three pernicious computer bugs. He upgraded the latest versions of all the programs he normally used. He ran diagnostics and corrected several corrupted files. He put a new ink cartridge in the printer. When he rebooted the computer, everything worked great. The man was so happy. The End.

The man with all the problems shrugged and would have continued to talk about his own problems, but his friend shook his head. "Think about the story I just told you," he said and walked off.

And the man with all the problems did. For days the story kept popping up in his thoughts and he pondered its meaning, but the story just didn't make sense. Why would his friend tell him this story? What did a computer have to do with his problems? And then it dawned on him. After his billionth fight with his teenaged daughter over her loud music, he realized there was a glitch in his relationship with her. They were stuck in the same place, having the same conversation over and over again. Then all the other glitches in his life became apparent. He laid on his bed and cried like a baby. When he couldn't cry anymore, he realized that *he* was the computer in the story. He needed diagnostic work and a reboot.

Going to the therapist was painful. Changing his diet was hard work. He thought the exercise plan the physician recommended would kill him. But he started enjoying his kids again. He took them places and did things with them. His wife was thrilled when he helped with chores. Through it all he thought about that malfunctioning computer. Eventually he would fix those pesky glitches.

Judicial parables work when hearers compare their own situations with those described in the parable. This comparison is necessarily metaphorical. The man compared his life to the broken computer and gained insight into solving his own problems. The broken computer was a metaphor for his life. His friend could have advised him concerning everything he should be doing differently, and perhaps he already had. However, the metaphorical realization that he *himself* was the broken computer became the catalyst that led to his newfound health.

Judicial parables don't always work instantly. Sometimes they need to rattle around the hearer's subconscious awhile. Sometimes judicial parables don't work at all. But, when they do, the results are often dramatic and life changing.

One of the most famous examples of a judicial parable effecting change in an individual is found in the Hebrew Bible.

The Parable of the Ewe Lamb

And the LORD sent Nathan to David. He came to him, and said to him, "There were two men in a certain city, the one rich and the other poor. The rich man had very many flocks and herds, but the poor man had nothing but one little ewe lamb, which he had bought. He brought it up, and it grew up with him and with his children; it used to eat of his meager fare, and drink from his cup, and lie in his bosom, and it was like a daughter to him. Now there came a traveler to the rich man, and he was loath to take one of his own flock or herd to prepare for the wayfarer who had come to him, but he took the poor man's lamb, and prepared that for the guest who had come to him."

Then David's anger was greatly kindled against the man. He said to Nathan, "As the LORD lives, the man who has done this deserves to die; he shall restore the lamb fourfold, because he did this thing, and because he had no pity."

Nathan said to David, "You are the man!"

...David said to Nathan, "I have sinned against the LORD." (2 Sam 12:1–7a, 13)

In this case, the judicial parable worked instantly. Let's look at the parable's context to see why it functioned so effectively.

Nathan was an eleventh-century BCE prophet who served King David. David was popular and deeply religious, but he had faults. He committed adultery with Bathsheba, the wife of one of his soldiers. When she became pregnant by David, he arranged to have her husband, Uriah, murdered in battle. Then, David married Bathsheba (Uriah's widow) to cover up his own sin of adultery. Here was Nathan's dilemma. There was a disparity of power between the two. David was king while Nathan was only a minor religious official. God commanded Nathan to deliver a stinging message of rebuke to David that included the announcement that Bathsheba's infant would die. If Nathan delivered this divine message in the conventional manner, there was a chance David would react violently and Nathan would be killed. If Nathan didn't deliver the message, he was in violation of his promise to be faithful to God. Nathan was dead if he did and damned if he didn't.

Nathan knew David had a reputation for being unpredictable and even violent when a messenger announced the death of someone David loved. The messenger who announced Saul's death was executed on the spot (2 Sam 1:14–16). Rechab and Baanah were executed when they told David they had assassinated Saul's son, Ishbosheth (2 Sam 4:9–12). Even though all three of these messengers had expected to be rewarded, David did not want to be associated with those who had assassinated his rivals. We don't know if there were other circumstances where David killed messengers for announcing bad news, as the Hebrew Bible is only a spotty source of history. Nathan might have been privy to other stories not passed down, but these two examples were enough to give any messenger delivering bad news to David cause for making funeral pre-arrangements.

Nathan's task was made even more difficult by the sensitive nature of the information he possessed. David's sins were *not* common knowledge. Only Joab and a handful of trusted guards and servants knew the details of what had taken place. David had worked discreetly so the people of Israel would never know he was guilty of adultery and murder. Nathan's announcement of God's punishment would open up David's reign to an embarrassing scandal. Nathan might have been unsure just how many people David was willing to murder to keep the scandal secret.

Furthermore, Nathan knew David's sins were not accidental or done in a single moment of weakness. When Bathsheba became pregnant, David intentionally arranged to have Uriah murdered; then he married Bathsheba to complete the cover-up. David had willfully and calculatingly committed adultery *and* murder. David knew the commandments; he knew he had sinned. Nathan didn't need to explain that David had broken the sixth and seventh commandments. David knew, and by the calculating way he continued to act, seemed not to care.

Nathan's task was not to educate David about sin, but to inspire David to repent and seek forgiveness. Nathan's chance of success was diminished if he approached the issue directly. The task would go completely unaccomplished if Nathan's blood was spilled on the floor after a direct confrontation with the king. Therefore, Nathan sought an indirect way to deal with the issue. The danger Nathan faced cannot be underestimated. This story was recorded and celebrated precisely because of its success. If David had failed to fall into the trap, we would know nothing about this ancient scandal and would find Nathan in an unmarked grave. But Nathan was successful.

Knowing that David had been a shepherd before becoming king, Nathan crafted a story about a poor slaughtered lamb so the same justice issues were at stake while the identity of the perpetrator was obscured. The parable features a poor man wronged by a rich man. Such a pauper would have trouble getting justice at the city gate where small claims court was held. The timing of Nathan's parable was likely the day the king heard appeals from court cases that could not be settled by the elders at the city gates. That a religious leader brought a case of injustice to the king was not unusual: Nathan may have advocated for other mistreated souls before. Perhaps that's how Nathan originally got the idea for his parable. As Nathan explained how the rich man with many sheep had stolen and slaughtered the only ewe lamb who was like a pet to the poor man, David got angry. David could relate to the story. He knew how lambs could become like pets, and he knew how callously the rich could treat the poor. "As the Lord lives, the man who has done this deserves to die," David exclaimed. To which Nathan replied, "You are the man."

By approaching David's sins indirectly through the parable, Nathan was able to scale the protective walls David had built to guard his heart from the knowledge he had murdered a man so he could steal his wife. The poor man's ewe and Uriah's wife were laid out "side by side" so that in the span of a moment David was able to experience the pain he had caused and was able to take responsibility for his actions. "I have sinned against the Lord," David replied. Nathan's speech of judgment would have fallen on deaf ears if David had been unable to lay the poor man's ewe side by side with Uriah's wife. The ending could have been different if that spark of recognition had not happened inside David when Nathan announced, "You are the man."

Nathan's plan was effective for three reasons. First, he knew David well enough to craft the parable with familiar characters: a rich man, a poor man, and a pet ewe lamb callously slaughtered. Second, he delivered the parable in the appeal court context knowing David would pass judgment. Third, David's sins were parallel with those of the rich man in the parable so David would immediately make the connection when it was pointed out.

The earlier parable of the broken computer functioned as a judicial parable when the problem-laden man saw the connection between his life and the broken computer. His friend told him the parable and walked off. The friend left the process open ended.

There was no hurry for the situation to be brought to resolution. The parable worked when it worked.

The parable of the ewe lamb was used as the bait in a judicial trap. In practice, judicial parable traps are difficult to pull off. Three conditions must be met for a judicial parable trap to be effective: First, hearers will only be caught in the trap if they believe the story actually happened or is plausibly true. If they think the story is hypothetical, the way the situation resolved is also hypothetical and cannot be taken seriously. Second, hearers must not prematurely detect the similarity between the parable and their own crimes. The parable teller has to strike a careful balance between getting too close to the parable's application and being too remote from it. If the teller speaks of a crime too close to the hearers' crimes, hearers will be less likely to be harsh in passing judgment and the parable's effectiveness is undermined. However, if the teller narrates a crime too distant from the hearers' crimes, the hearers might not perceive the connection and the parable isn't effective either. And, third, hearers of the parable have to be enticed to pass a judgment upon the crime in the parable. Unless hearers give an opinion about what should be done about the perpetrator of the parable's crime, the parable can't be used to judge the hearers' crimes. The whole point of the judicial parable trap is to have people judge themselves with the same judgment they apply to others. Because most people are apt to judge their own sins more leniently than the same sins committed by others, some way has to be designed to help them put their own crimes into perspective. If they don't take the bait and condemn the crime described in the parable, then that same judgment cannot be offered back to them as their own punishment.

Timing is essential for parable traps to be sprung effectively. The right parable told at the wrong moment will be ineffective. The teller only gets one chance with a particular parable to trap the hearer. Once the hearer suspects he has been targeted, he is less likely to let the parable slip past his guard. For these reasons, judicial parable traps should be used sparingly, and especially in circumstances when there is a disparity of power between the teller and hearer and direct conversation has previously failed or would be ineffective.

There are five examples of judicial parable traps in the Hebrew Bible. Two of them were told against King David: Nathan's parable, and one told by a woman of Tekoa to entice David to forgive his son Absalom (2 Sam 14). A third parable is told by one of the prophets against King Ahab for being too merciful in his war with the Arameans (1 Kgs 20:35–43). The final two judicial parables were used by Isaiah (Isa 5:1–7) and Jeremiah (Jer 3:1–5) against the sinful people of Israel.

In a congregational context, religious leaders can use open-ended judicial parables in counseling and teaching settings where there is an atmosphere of mutual love and trust. Like the man with personal problems who was told the parable of the broken computer, people are seeking to resolve their problems and *do* welcome the religious leader's attempt to help them, even if a particular parable takes a while to work or even if they don't get it in the end. That the religious leader cares about them and is trying to help them find insight is powerful, even if the leader's individual attempts at inspiring insight do not always work. The same is true with judicial parable traps. Used in a context of love and trust with people who are truly interested in growth, they can be very effective.

However, be very wary using any judicial parables with people who oppose the religious leader's ministry or who are firmly set in their life course and are actively resistant to change. People like this are hungry alligators lying peacefully in the still water. Provoke them by implying they need spiritual growth and you won't be able to run fast enough from those snapping jaws and thrashing tails. The wise religious leader must use discernment to determine which method of inspiring spiritual growth is right for each individual person. Most people are able to be reached by directly addressing their problems with possible solutions. Others are reached metaphorically through parables. But, like the alligator, some people are best left alone altogether unless the religious leader is specially prepared for the dangers that might follow.

Teaching-Metaphor Parables

The Parable of the Snake

"Grasped wrongly," said the Buddha on a certain occasion, "the Scriptures conduce to hurt and harm."

It is precisely as if a man, wanting a water-snake, hunting a water-snake, searching for a water-snake, were to see a big water-snake and were to grasp it by the body or by the tail, and that water-snake were to turn on him and were to bite him on the hand or on the arm or on some other major or minor member of the body, and as a result of this he were to incur death or mortal pain. And why? Because he wrongly grasped the water-snake.

"Precisely so," said the Buddha, "the Scriptures, wrongly grasped, conduce to hurt and harm."

"On the other hand," said the Buddha, "the Scriptures, rightly grasped, conduce to weal and welfare."

It is precisely as if a man, wanting a water-snake, hunting a water-snake, searching for a water-snake, were to see a big water-snake, and with a goat's foot, with a stick, were to hold it down, were to hold it down firmly; and with the goat's foot, with the stick, holding it down, holding it down firmly, were to grasp it by the neck, were to grasp it firmly—no matter how much that water-snake were to wrap its coils about that man's hand or arm or other major or minor member of his body, nevertheless, as a result of that man's firm grasp, he would incur neither death nor mortal pain. And why? Because he rightly grasped the water-snake.

"Precisely so," said the Buddha, "the Scriptures, rightly grasped, conduce to weal and welfare."[1]

While judicial parables inspire change, teaching-metaphor parables inspire insight into confusing subjects. The Buddha's students couldn't understand how scripture could be harmful. If scripture is good and valuable for teaching, how could it harm someone? Clearly, the deductive teaching method whereby the teacher stated the correct answer and asked students to accept that answer was not effective in this case. The concept of scripture being harmful was an advanced lesson not easily grasped. To increase comprehension, Buddha selected a metaphor familiar to the students. The metaphor was not the snake itself, but the process of catching the snake. The entire story was the metaphor. When catching a snake was compared to the real-life problem of grasping scriptures correctly, the students benefitted from the comparison and learned the intended lesson. Sometimes if scriptures are grasped incorrectly, harm can follow.

The teaching-metaphor parable has a different function than the judicial parable. All the subconscious processes whereby judicial parables inspire change work the same with teaching-metaphor parables, except the result is insight instead of a decision to change. Unlike judicial parable traps, which work only if the parable teller's motives are obscured, teaching-metaphor parables require no secretiveness. Teachers can be honest about their motives to inspire insight. They can either let students induce which object should be compared with the parable, or they can supply it and help students dissect the metaphor and shape their conclusion. Both are examples of the inductive teaching method.

In the inductive teaching method, the teacher provides samples for students to examine. Students struggle with the similarities and differences of these samples and induce a conclusion based upon their observations. This can be done in two different ways.

1. In a *guided inductive lesson,* the teacher asks leading questions and confirms conclusions so students will arrive at the place the teacher desires.
2. In an *unguided inductive lesson,* the teacher does not interfere in the development of the students' conclusions.

Parables can be used either way in the classroom. The deductive method, on the other hand, starts with the conclusion and provides examples to defend it. Students don't have to struggle; they just have to memorize. Because the inductive method forces students to think for themselves, there is a greater chance for long-term retention of the lesson. This is the beauty of using parables as teaching metaphors.

Grasping the scriptures wrongly is as much a problem in all world religions today as it was among Buddha's followers in his day. Islamic fundamentalists misunderstand the Qur'ān and declare jihad on their enemies. Both liberal and conservative Christians twist the meaning of the Bible to justify their own viewpoints. Scriptures are being used in ways that pervert the holy teachings. "The Parable of the Snake" helps religious people think about scripture in a more complex way. While reading scripture is good and life-giving, reading scripture inappropriately creates problems that can cause harm to the religious community. All religious people need to keep this concept in mind when they approach their own scriptures, whether that be the *Lotus Sutra,* the Qur'ān, or the Bible.

Used as teaching metaphors, parables powerfully make complicated concepts accessible. Obscure theological concepts, difficult to explain with propositions, become easier to grasp when explained metaphorically through the use of parables. Teachers do not need to hide their intentions when using parables as teaching metaphors. They can openly state the intended comparison or guide students to it. Both are equally effective in using parables as teaching metaphors.

Example-Metaphor Parables

The Parable of the Good Samaritan

Just then a lawyer stood up to test Jesus. "Teacher," he said, "what must I do to inherit eternal life?" He said to him, "What is written in the law? What do you read there?" He answered, "You shall love the Lord your God with all your heart, and with all your strength, and with all your mind; and your neighbor as yourself." And he said to him, "You have given the right answer; do this, and you will live."

But wanting to justify himself, he asked Jesus, "And who is my neighbor?" Jesus replied, "A man was going down from Jerusalem to Jericho, and fell into the hands of robbers, who stripped him, beat him, and went away, leaving him half dead. Now by chance a priest was going down that road; and when he saw him, he passed by on the other side. So likewise a Levite, when he came to the place and saw him, passed by on the other side. But a Samaritan while traveling came near him; and when he saw him, he was moved with pity. He went to him and bandaged his wounds, having poured oil and wine on them. Then he put him on his own animal, brought him to an inn, and took care of him. The next day he took out two denarii, gave them to the innkeeper, and said, 'Take care of him; and when I come back, I will repay you whatever more you spend.' Which of these three, do you think, was a neighbor to the man who fell into the hands of the robbers?" He said, "The one who showed him mercy." Jesus said to him, "Go and do likewise." (Luke 10:25–37)

The example-metaphor parable is also told to teach something new, but the goal is not to inspire insight but to provide students with a concrete model to imitate. In "The Parable of the Good Samaritan," the lawyer asked Jesus to clarify who was his neighbor. If the question had been an honest one, Jesus could have told a teaching-metaphor parable to provide insight, but the question was designed to *trap* Jesus into saying something contrary to the law. Clearly, the lawyer was able to quote from the law and knew the answer. He was hoping to incite Jesus to say something contradictory. By telling this particular parable, Jesus was not trying to provide an insightful answer to a superfluous question, but was giving the people overhearing this conversation an example to imitate. The key to understanding Jesus's motive for telling the story is found in his final response, "Go and do likewise." He didn't say, "I hope this answers your question," or "I hope this clarifies the concept of neighbor." Jesus wanted people to model the behavior of the story's hero.

And, as an example metaphor, "The Parable of the Good Samaritan" is particularly well done. The twist in the parable comes when, after both a Jewish priest and a Jewish Levite ignore the injured man (who is assumed to be Jewish), a man from Samaria, a traditional enemy of Jews, provides assistance. The story is effective for Jews because if a *Samaritan* can provide neighborly assistance, why can't Jews offer the same to each other? According to Jewish law, even resident aliens and travelers were to be extended hospitality. Jesus didn't teach anything new, but made the existing law accessible so people could go out and literally "do likewise."

Example-metaphor parables are used when students understand an esoteric concept intellectually but are unable to implement that concept in practice. Real-life problems that could be solved using example-metaphor parables might include talking to your own children about sex, apologizing to a friend, disciplining an errant employee, starting a personal recycling program, making time to exercise, or getting involved in a community organization. In each case, an individual understands the concept needing action, but may lack courage or practical information to proceed. The example-metaphor parable bridges the gap between knowledge and application. Within the context of religious organizations, example-metaphor parables can be used to help redefine roles that already have a long history. A parable can help people adapt to a new model of doing old tasks.

The Parable of the Too Young Usher

"I'm sixteen! I am old enough to be an usher," the youth exclaimed loudly. "Just let me try one Sunday and I'll show you I can be the best usher this church has ever had."

The three gray-haired old men frowned and looked at each other uncomfortably. One pointed his cane at the youth and said, "Ushers set examples for the congregation. You must be serious and do the task with dignity and decorum. You have to be a servant of the people."

The pastor walked up and intervened before the young man could reply. "Since we have an opening for an usher now that

John has died, why don't you let Dwayne give it a try. I think it's an excellent idea for some of our younger members to serve."

The old men eyed each other uncomfortably and then nodded as a group.

"Be here an hour early next Sunday. Don't be late!" one of the men barked gruffly.

The next Sunday Dwayne was sitting on the church's doorstep when the three old men hobbled up to unlock the door thirty minutes before service began. Dwayne was enthusiastic. Having watched the ushers perform their duties before, he quickly added oil to the altar candles, changed the paraments on the communion table and pulpit to the right color, folded the last of the bulletins, and eagerly greeted the first worshipers as they entered the sanctuary. Dwayne met the Nelson family at the curb and carried their diaper bag down to the nursery for them as they brought in the twins. He reparked Mrs. Johnson's car for her when she couldn't get it between the lines, and then escorted her to her seat on the third pew, right corner. When a visitor came in, the old ushers ignored her, but Dwayne greeted her enthusiastically and made a special effort to introduce her by name to the pastor. Dwayne made sure all the children had freshly sharpened crayons and a good supply of take-home coloring sheets to help them make it through the service. He petitioned that one of the children be allowed to light the candles and was begrudgingly allowed to oversee that task.

After the service began, the three old ushers whispered to themselves in their traditional seats next to the back wall. When little Johnny had to go to the restroom before the second hymn, Dwayne offered to escort him so his mom wasn't inconvenienced. Dwayne did a security walk-through of the building and got back just in time to hear the sermon. The three old ushers were deep in conversation. When Mr. Parker started his weekly coughing fit, Dwayne brought him a glass of water.

After the service, the pastor commented on how good a job Dwayne had done. One of the old ushers nodded begrudgingly and added, "He's still got a lot to learn."

"Being an usher is easy," Dwayne said with pride. "You just have to know the people and serve them with love."

In "The Parable of the Too Young Usher," the traditional role of usher in a small congregation is contrasted with a new possibility for how that role can be adapted. Hearers of the parable are able to see new possibilities for the role of usher, and new or existing ushers are able to model the parable by being more actively involved in the servant role of helping a congregation be more comfortable, hopefully providing them a better opportunity to be actively engaged in worship. Usher training could easily be done in a more traditional format. An usher check-off sheet could be provided that lists all the weekly tasks that must be accomplished by the ushers. A lecture could ensue. Using the parable as a component of usher training allows for a discussion to occur about what it means to be a loving servant of the congregation. The comparison between the old ushers and Dwayne contrasts the old passive model with a newer more active one.

Anti-Example-Metaphor Parables

A subtype of example-metaphor parables is the anti-example-metaphor. In an anti-example-metaphor parable, the story becomes an example of what *not* to do. Look at the following example.

The Parable of the Man Who Mastered the First Date

There was a man who considered himself the master of the first date. He had been on hundreds of first dates. One day a coworker asked him his technique. "Easy," he replied. "Always show up late. Women like to be kept waiting. Flowers are trite. Many women are allergic to them anyway. Don't bother with flowers. Candy makes them fat, so don't bring candy. I always insist that dinner costs be paid by her. Since I asked her out, she should pay. And, boy do I like exotic and expensive food! Dinner conversation should always be about me. I want her to get to know me. I tell her all about my other dates and why they weren't the right girl for me. That way she will know how to please me. I never give her compliments. I wouldn't want her to get an inflated ego. After dinner, I like to take her someplace unusual. Everybody goes to a movie. I'm certainly not everybody. One time we went out to the sewage treatment plant for a tour. Another time we took a romantic walk through the junkyard. I make sure all my dates are memorable so women will never forget me. That's the secret!"

The coworker remarked, "I bet you don't have many second dates."

"No, not a single one yet, but I'm the master of the first date!"

In "The Parable of the Man Who Mastered the First Date" the technique of exaggeration is used to describe a man who does absolutely everything wrong on a first date. The man's behavior is an anti-example for a first date. Rather than imitate his behavior, everything he did should be actively avoided. Anti-example-metaphor parables are effective because they reframe a situation from a reverse perspective. They often add humor, breaking down barriers and allowing for easier lesson absorption.

However, anti-example-metaphor parables should be used cautiously. While most people will easily recognize the parables as an anti-example and learn the inverse lesson, a few people will mistake them for examples. Impressionable children can imitate antiheroes to their detriment. Antiheroes are supposed to be villains whose personality characteristics should not be imitated. In old westerns, the villain always wore a black hat and was the object of disdain. Nobody wanted to be like him. The villain was never the main character, only a minor player in the drama centered around the hero in the white hat. However, the distinctions between heroes and villains have now become somewhat blurred as Hollywood has sought to portray heroes with character defects and villains with a few positive characteristics. Villains have even become main characters in many modern dramas. When villains were clearly labeled, they served as antiheroes, examples of how *not* to behave in society.

Much can be learned about appropriate behavior by studying anti-heroes. Unfortunately, a few children have mistaken antiheroes for heroes and, in the absence of parental figures to clarify their ideas, have learned the wrong lessons in life. Anti-example-metaphor parables can be very effective. However, they should be avoided with very young hearers or those who are in the beginning stages of learning about a subject. Nothing is more tragic than having an anti-example be mistaken for an example.

Because of their often comic nature, anti-example parables are often helpful in church situations when church members *know* what is right, but aren't *doing* it. Church meetings that go on forever because attendees would rather talk about football, greeters who socialize with everyone but visitors, readers who don't return church library books, and the realities of what church life would be like without vacation Bible school volunteers are all situations that readily lend themselves to correction using a comic anti-example parable. "The Parable of the Too Young Usher" is an example-metaphor parable in which hearers are expected to imitate the behavior of Dwayne. If the parable was adapted so that Dwayne did everything wrong, then the parable could still be used in usher training, but potential ushers would be expected to learn the inverse lesson. Use example-metaphor parables with beginners. With experienced leaders who need retraining or modification in their behaviors, use anti-example metaphor parables.

Discerning Parable Type in Real Applications

Since parable type is introduced *only* for teaching how parables work in practice, there is necessarily some ambiguity in discerning a particular parable's type apart from its original context. A particular parable may function differently if it is used in a different context. Likewise, while a parable teller might have a specific motive in relating a particular parable, hearers may receive it completely differently depending upon the hearers' own personal contexts. The excellent judicial parable designed to convict a wrongdoer of some sin might spark an insight into something completely unrelated. While the parable did not work in the judicial way intended, the teaching-metaphor function worked fine. Parable tellers lose control of the process after the parable has been spoken. The same parable might affect three different hearers, each according to a different type. The first hearer might be convicted of an improper relationship. The second hearer might gain insight into a topic she had never understood before. A third hearer might use the parable as an example to imitate. Parables are more like a shotgun shooting buckshot in a broad blast pattern than a sniper's rifle hitting a distant target. The unintended effect of indirect communication is that it can be received in a variety of ways. This can be an advantage. Let's look at an example from the Islamic Sufi tradition.

The Ancient Coffer of Nuri Bey

Nuri Bey was a reflective and respected Albanian who had married a wife much younger than himself.

One evening when he had returned home earlier than usual, a faithful servant came to him and said: "Your wife, our mistress, is acting suspiciously. She is in her apartments with a huge chest, large enough to hold a man, which belonged to your grandmother."

"It should contain only a few ancient embroideries."

"I believe that there may now be much more in it. She will not allow me, your oldest retainer, to look inside."

Nuri went to his wife's room, and found her sitting disconsolately beside the massive wooden box.

"Will you show me what is in the chest?" he asked.

"Because of the suspicion of a servant, or because you do not trust me?"

"Would it not be easier just to open it, without thinking about the undertones?" asked Nuri.

"I do not think it possible."

"Is it locked?"

"Yes."

"Where is the key?"

She held it up. "Dismiss the servant and I will give it to you."

The servant was dismissed. The woman handed over the key and herself withdrew, obviously troubled in mind.

Nuri Bey thought for a long time. Then he called four gardeners from his estate. Together they carried the chest by night unopened to a distant part of the grounds, and buried it.

The matter was never referred to again.[2]

This thirteenth-century parable is rich with meaning, and the context of the hearer will determine which moral speaks loudest. A man who distrusts his wife and is constantly snooping in her personal possessions looking for scandal might be convicted of his jealousy and decide to be more trusting. The parable functioned as a judicial parable in his context. A twice-divorced woman who had been in abusive relationships before might for the first time in her life gain insight into what it means to truly trust someone. The parable functioned as a teaching metaphor in her context. And a young couple just starting out their lives together might decide to use the parable as an example to imitate. They pledge not to pry, choosing to trust each other. The parable functioned as an example metaphor in their context.

The Covert Nature of How Parables Function

Parables do their job covertly in two distinct ways. First, parable tellers often obscure the purpose for telling particular parables. Humorists, on the other hand, signal their hearers when they are about to tell a joke. This is important because the intention to joke sanctions laughter as an acceptable response and overcomes any reservations about social expectations. Even if hearers don't "get" the punch line, they can respond with polite smiles. If humorists don't effectively signal their intention to joke, hearers might not be sure if laughter is appropriate. Humor is compromised if hearers are unaware of the intention to joke.[3] This is not the case with parables. Especially with judicial parables, announcing the intention "to parable" would destroy the transformative opportunity. Likewise with teaching-metaphor or example-metaphor parables, no advance warning is necessary for hearers to find insight. Parable tellers often use stories for teaching or transformative purposes by obscuring their motives. The parable is like an invisible bludgeon parable tellers use to strike hearers. Hearers don't see the blows fall, but feel their effects without knowing its source.

Second, parables act covertly on hearers by slipping past their cognitive defenses. Self-deceived individuals put up barriers to keep themselves from perceiving the truth. Parables allow the truth to be hidden in a story and subvert those internal barriers. Parables are Trojan horses. The story of the parable is a gift received with joy. But at night, when the subconscious has lowered its defenses, the hidden meaning sneaks out and opens the gate so insight can crash through the mind's protective walls. Parables are suitcase bombs. The suitcase of the parable's story is received as if it were harmless, and the suitcase is carried wherever the hearer goes. But, one day, the detonator within explodes, shooting into the soul the shrapnel of insight, meaning, and understanding. Parables are a gift package. The parable's story is the beautiful wrapping paper with the bow so carefully tied. The present is received with great anticipation as an entertaining moment of distraction. But the recipient does not know what is inside the gift box until it is opened, and then it is too late to return the parable's cutting message to the sender. Such is the covert nature of how parables act on hearers.

At first, when I heard the Buddha's preaching, there was great astonishment and doubt in my mind. Is this not a devil pretending to be the Buddha, trying to vex and confuse my mind? I thought. But the Buddha employed various causes, similes, and parables, expounding eloquently. His mind was peaceful as the sea, and as I listened, I was freed from the net of doubt. The Lotus Sutra[1]

4.

THE STYLISTIC ANATOMY OF A PARABLE

Parables are brief, metaphorically shocking stories. Metaphors are a "figure of speech, in which one thing, idea, or action is referred to by a word or expression normally denoting another thing, idea or action, so as to suggest some common quality shared by the two."[2] In short, metaphors draw a comparison between two subjects. In the simple metaphor "Love is a rose," the two subjects are laid side by side for simple comparison. In parables, the metaphorical comparison is often obscured by a literary device in order to keep the hearer from making the connection too quickly. In the case of judicial parables, hearers tend to be one of the subjects in the comparison, so tellers want the *entire* metaphor to be laid out before hearers are able to recognize the intended comparison so hearers won't prematurely reject the parable's hidden meaning. In the case of teaching-metaphor and example-metaphor parables, the two subjects tend to be complex. Delaying the metaphorical comparison can aid in understanding because hearers aren't able to make the comparison too quickly and dismiss its implications prematurely.

Often, the second subject in the metaphorical comparison is left ambiguous. The first subject is the parable itself. Hearers are then left to struggle with what in their *own* lives makes the second subject. In the hearers' struggle to find the second referent, parables are able to provoke the subconscious mind into action, allowing hearers to find hidden insight into themselves or into an unknown subject. The art of parable construction is in the ability to obscure the metaphorical comparison enough to require deep thought, but not so much that a comparison cannot be made. There are a variety of ways parables can be constructed to accomplish this goal. We will call the literary device that both makes and obscures the metaphorical comparison the literary *style* of the parable. The *type* of the parable is how it functions on hearers. The *style* of the parable is the internal literary construction that aids the metaphorical comparison. There are three basic types of parable and fifteen common literary styles used in parable construction. These may not be the only styles possible, but they are certainly the most common.

Parables may adhere to only a single literary style, but they don't have to. Two or more literary devices might be at work simultaneously in a given parable. In the same way that a building can use more than one style of architectural construction to give it a hybrid appearance, literary constructions can be blended together to form hybrid styles. These styles are explored primarily to learn about how parables are constructed. Hearers tend to be less concerned about knowing how a parable is put together as they are with its overall effectiveness in providing insight. Likewise, homeowners are more concerned about how their home functions than whether it was put together with nails, screws, or bolts.

This chapter provides an overview of how literary style influences the usefulness of parables in general situations.

The Tale

The Parable of the Wizard and the Tropical Fish

There was a great wizard who loved tropical fish. So he built a huge aquarium out of glass. He lined the bottom with the finest gravel and planted seaweed and other beautiful plants there for the fish to enjoy. He installed an aeration system and a temperature controller. After filling the aquarium with water, the great wizard lovingly introduced several varieties of tropical fish.

Day after day, the great wizard fed the fish from his own hand by sprinkling the food across the top of the water in the tank. As the food slowly sank toward the bottom, the fish would dart in and out from around the seaweed, quickly eating the tiny pellets. But the fish did not know who fed them. Weekly, the wizard would change a portion of the water so the aquarium would remain healthy. The fish were frightened by the turmoil in their environment. The great wizard had no way of comforting them. The wizard maintained the aquarium heater and the aerator, but the tropical fish did not realize who it was who provided these necessities for them.

The great wizard loved his tropical fish, but he had no way of communicating that love to them except to continually care for them. One day, the great wizard's love became so great for his fish that he decided to tell them of his love personally. So, he turned himself into a fish and entered the tank so he could tell them in their own language. Let the one who has ears hear.

The *tale,* or simple story, is one of the oldest and most common literary styles used for parables. The *tale style* is included in this list precisely because it sets the standard for parable form. A tale is a narrative story that has a distinct beginning, middle, and end. Of course, for it to be a parabolic story, there has to be a metaphorical comparison and a surprising twist. As a tale, "The Parable of the Wizard and the Tropical Fish" has a distinct beginning, middle, and end. In this particular case each of the three paragraphs represents the three progressive movements in the tale. We have already noted that in the single sentence parable of the mustard seed that a distinct beginning, middle, and end was present, so there is flexibility in implementation. The ordering of the three is not particularly important either, since a tale can be told with the end first, followed by the beginning and middle. However, if the tale is missing one of these three parts, its style is no longer that of the tale. As will be shown later in the chapter, a parable with no ending is an *unfinished tale style*, and a parable with only a middle is a *slice of life style*.

The tale style is frequently found in response to a question. "Why would God become a human?" might be the question for which "The Parable of the Wizard and the Tropical Fish" is the answer. Tale style parables attributed to both Jesus and Buddha have been associated with questions asked by either followers or detractors. (Scholars sometimes argue about whether later editors tinkered with the questions associated with given parables, but that is outside the scope of this study.) For our purposes, the tale lends itself to providing an answer to a difficult question without having the answer be too limiting or too simple. Parables with other styles can also be used to answer questions, but the tale is most associated with the question context.

Slice of Life

The Lost Penny

"I'd be glad to front you some start-up capital for a business," the older man said. "Or, if you'd prefer, I could put in a good word for you at the plant. I could promise you $15.00 per hour plus benefits."

The younger man kicked a stone that had wandered up onto the sidewalk. This was the first evening walk he'd taken with his uncle in years. When he had been a boy, they had frequently taken walks in the woods. As his uncle got older and his business had increased, the frequent walks in the woods became occasional walks in the city park, then had ceased altogether. The western sky was just beginning to take on an orange hue as the sun was threatening to set. A warm breeze stirred the leaves in the trees ever so slightly.

"Uncle, I appreciate the offer, but I'm really happy at my job. I'm doing what I enjoy."

"Nonsense! How can you be happy baking donuts and wedding cakes? The pay can't be more than minimum wage. How will you support a family?"

Tom kicked another stone and watched it bounce down the sidewalk before answering. "I make enough to get by. It's not the money that's important. Before I start my shift I take a walk in the woods behind the bakery and listen to the crickets and watch the night sky. There's hardly a day goes by that I don't see a shooting star or one of the planets zooming through the sky. And after that, I walk into the bakery and smell the fresh dough, cookies baking, and coffee. It's a wonderful feeling."

"But, Tom, you have to start thinking about the future."

"Yes, uncle, but it was you who taught me to appreciate the beauty of nature. I'm happy. Let's just leave it at that."

The older man stopped suddenly and pointed at an errant penny slipped from someone's pocket. "Pick it up. It'll bring you good luck."

Tom kicked another stone. "I don't need the luck today. My life is great already. I've got everything I need to make me happy."

"A little extra luck won't hurt anyone."

"Then you pick it up. Your business has grown so that you don't even have time to take long walks in the woods. A little extra luck would do *you* good."

Tom was already ten yards ahead, but his uncle hadn't budged. The older man replied, "Seriously, 'A penny saved is a penny earned.' Pick it up."

Tom turned around and walked backward away from his uncle. "I don't need it. Besides, some young child will come along and pick it up and be thrilled. Let them have that joyful experience."

"How can you walk away and leave money like that?"

"Come along, uncle. It's only a penny. It won't buy anything anymore."

Reluctantly, the old man walked on, although he looked back twice. They walked in silence for a long time listening to the ball games in progress on two of the three ballfields. The sun sank a bit lower and the field lights began to pop on one at a time. Finally, the old man broke the silence, "Pennies add up you know."

Tom laughed. "Are you still fretting over that penny?" Tom looked at his uncle and saw the deadly seriousness of his face. "This really bothers you doesn't it?"

The older man nodded.

"You're worth millions of dollars, uncle, and you're still brooding over a penny that you didn't earn. Do you own the wealth, or does the wealth own you?"

"Pennies add up, Tom. You're missing the point."

"No, I think *you're* missing the point. You worry over pennies that don't belong to you and don't spend enough time wandering in the woods. You may be very rich, but I'm richer in what really counts. You taught me that long ago. Only now, you've forgotten."

The *slice of life style* is simply a single scene that hearers get to observe and contemplate. It is a single slice of someone's day or life. Usually, the slice is that of an ordinary situation that has an unusual twist that makes the scene memorable. In "The Lost Penny," the happy but poor nephew refused to pick up a penny to add to his coffer, while the wealthy uncle obsessed about it. One would expect the opposite. In this particular slice of life, insight is gained into the concept of wealth. Wealth is not about how much you have, but how happy you are with what you've got. The scene encourages hearers to lay their own concept of wealth next to either Tom's or the rich uncle's. Not every slice of life is parabolic. The secret to making this style work is in choosing the right slice of life that has meaning above the ordinary.

Not every single-scene parable embodies *slice of life* either. Rather, the ordinariness of the scene, along with the twist that makes the scene extraordinary, is what sets this type of parable apart from other literary devices. Slice of life parables do not require a beginning or an end. The middle of the story, the slice, is what is important. Only background information relevant to that particular slice of life needs to be introduced to assist hearers in understanding the scene. The slice of life type might be thought of as a tale style with no beginning or end, only the middle.

The Unfinished Tale

The Parable of the Unplanned Pregnancy

As it happened, Julie found out she was pregnant and was caught up in the dilemma of what to do about this awkward situation. She was nineteen, a college sophomore, with no husband, and not even a steady boyfriend. In this moment of crisis, she turned to two of her friends for advice.

Marge argued convincingly that she should have an abortion. Julie was too young to support a child, the father would likely run when he found out the news and would be no help, and raising a child in college would mean postponing her career.

Sophia argued equally well that bringing a life into the world was an endeavor every bit as valuable as having a career. The child would bring joy into her life. Her parents would likely be supportive, and there were a multitude of programs to help young single mothers finish their educations. Thus, Julie should keep the baby.

Marge countered that an abortion was easier and that Julie wasn't ready for the responsibility of caring for another person right now. After Julie got settled in her career and had a stable marriage relationship, then having a child made sense. Why would she want to complicate her life unnecessarily? Marge invited Julie to go with her to the abortion clinic and set up an appointment.

Sophia added that Julie would likely experience guilt if she had an abortion, and that guilt would plague her the rest of her life. If she didn't want to keep the child, she could easily put it up for adoption, and the adopted parents would likely even pay for the medical costs associated with the pregnancy. Sophia said she would help Julie set up an appointment at the local adoption center to look at her options.

Julie was grateful for the advice she received. She hugged both friends and indicated she was ready to set up that appointment.

The *unfinished tale style* is simply a tale without a proper ending. The surprising twist in the story is usually the abrupt cliff-hanging ending that leaves the tale unresolved. While this is usually unsatisfying for hearers who are listening solely for entertainment, the abrupt stoppage causes many hearers to critically reflect upon the story and supply their own endings. The unfinished tale style is good for presenting options and requiring hearers to choose between them. In "The Parable of the Unplanned Pregnancy," Julie's two friends provided information on abortion, both pro and con. The narrator of the parable appears to be neutral. Hearers are left to decide which appointment Julie made, with the abortion clinic or the adoption agency. There are no clues in the story itself that would allow hearers to authoritatively state that one option was preferred by Julie over the other. The parable becomes a discussion starter on a very controversial issue. By using this parable, the parable's teller has raised the controversial issue of abortion without tipping his hand as to what he believes is right and instead inspires hearers to argue about the issue itself. The unfinished tale style lends itself well to starting discussions on controversial issues.

Allegory

The Parable of the Mediocre Life

Mr. Mediocre was an average man, living an average life in the city of Typical. He had dreams for the future, but he never set goals or a time line to bring those dreams to fruition. He had the opportunity to date Miss Knockout, but the relationship didn't last. He didn't have the patience to deal with her constant primping and appetite for fine fashion. He finally broke it off when she suggested he could do something about his beer belly. He married Miss Dumpy instead and they had three Mediocre kids.

Mr. Mediocre had a pet peeve about incompetent people. At work he was always riding Mrs. Slacker and Mr. Screwup about their poor job performance. He also complained about Mrs. Innovative and Mr. Brilliant. They just couldn't seem to go along with what everyone else was doing, which made them incompetent in his eyes. Their ideas so galled him that he finally had to take his concerns to Mr. Bigshotboss who promptly fired them both.

Mr. Mediocre enjoyed sports—not playing them, but watching them on television. Mr. Jock was his favorite football player. He had an average career, but it wasn't his fault. If only that stupid coach, Mr. Hothead, would let him play more often the team would easily make the playoffs every year. Instead, Mr. Hothead allowed Mr. Superstar to play every game. Clearly, he wasn't worth the money they paid him. Anyone could see that.

Mr. Mediocre wasn't much of a religious man, but he went to church just in case there really was a God. He attended more than some and less than others. He figured that should guarantee him a spot in heaven, if there was such a place. In politics, he favored the Selfish Party over the Community Living Party. He wasn't a particular fan of art, but he didn't object to paintings by Mrs. Sentimental. On the other hand, he greatly disliked anything by Mr. Makemethink. Mr. Mediocre was a member of the Beerdrinkers Social Club because he thought he should be involved in the community. They met regularly, churned out a slew of minutes, but didn't require him to do any real work in the community.

One day Mr. Mediocre died of a heart attack. His family missed him. Fortunately, his three children grew up to be just like him. Mr. Mediocre would have been so proud.

The English word *allegory* is simply the transliteration of the Greek word *allegoria,* which nominally means "a description of one thing under the image of another." Allegorical writings were used as early as the fifth century BCE and have been popular ever since. John Bunyan's *The Pilgrim's Progress* is one of the most famous examples of allegory, but many examples abound and new ones are even being produced in the twenty-first century.

A parable that uses allegory is a story for which substitutions have been made throughout the story that refer to something other than what is literally stated in the story. In "The Parable of the Mediocre Life," the main character's surname is more than just a name: "Mediocre" describes the man's character. Each snippet of Mr. Mediocre's life in the parable illustrates the mediocrity of his very being. All of the people in the parable have names that allegorically anticipate their character. Without having any other supporting evidence, hearers can assume that Mrs. Innovative is a problem solver who can think outside the box, while Mr. Screwup makes lots of mistakes. People act according to their names in an allegory. Hearers who do not see the allegorical connection between the characters' names and the way they behave enjoy a simple story that is a little odd, but they miss the larger meaning of the parable as a whole: mediocrity is damaging to life.

For allegory to work properly, hearers must already be familiar with the concept being allegorized. Allegory can only pass on hidden information to the initiated.[3] Allegories tease hearers' minds into seeing something they already knew from a different point of view. Because allegories require prior knowledge of the subject being allegorized, this literary style is not a good choice for teaching new concepts to students.

According to Dan Otto Via, "In an allegory the elements in the story not only represent but are identical with their referents; therefore, they behave not according to their own logic or nature but according to the logic of what they represent. This means that an allegory is likely to contain improbabilities too great to be assimilated into the story; it will appear as nonsensical if read on its own terms and will have to be translated into what it represents in order to have sense made of it."[4] In "The Parable of the Mediocre Life," Mr. Bigshotboss fires Mrs. Innovative and Mr. Brilliant based solely upon the complaint of Mr. Mediocre. This action is not so much realistic of workplace protocol as it is symbolic of the mediocre worker's jealousy toward those who are innovative or brilliant.

"The Parable of the Mediocre Life" also makes use of the tale style.

Paradox

The Parable of the Inexperienced Applicant

The young man handed his completed employment application to the director of human resources. The director looked it over quickly and noted that the young man had no experience. He handed the application back and said, "No experience; no job."

The young man's countenance fell. "But how can I get experience if no one will give me a job? I've tried a dozen places already and they've all said the same thing."

"Tough luck kid. We don't have a sufficient profit margin to bother training someone from scratch."

The young man did not turn to go as expected. Instead, he asked, "Are your employees simply machines used to perform a specific task?"

The director shifted uncomfortably in his chair. "We expect our employees to perform a task and do it well. I wouldn't call them machines."

The young man pointed to the sign on the director's door. "The sign says 'Director of Human Resources.' If you are only interested in an employee's output, shouldn't the sign read 'Director of Machines'?"

Again the director shifted positions. "We provide benefits, paid vacation, sick leave, and a flexible work schedule. As director of human resources, I care about our employees as people."

A tear welled up in the young man's eyes. "Why don't you care about me then? The ad in the newspaper says you need help. I want to work. In fact, I might even become the best employee you've ever had. Why won't you invest in my potential by giving me a little on-the-job training?"

The director crossed his arms and answered, "Because you might not turn out to be capable of doing the job. If we hire experienced workers, we already know they can do the job."

"But how can someone like me with good references, a good education, and a good work ethic get experience if no one will hire me until I have experience?"

"You got me there kid. But, whatever you say, I'm still not going to hire you without experience."

Technically, a paradox is a statement that seems contradictory or absurd, but in reality might actually be true. In "The Parable of the Inexperienced Applicant," the paradox at work is inexperienced applicants can't get certain jobs without experience, but they can't get experience without having a job. Which comes first: the experience or the job? In the employment world, this is a paradoxical situation that nearly everyone has faced at one time or another. The parable explores the reasons certain employers require experience, but also raises the issue of the nature of employment itself. Are employees valued only for their labor and what they can do for the company? Or does the company have a more important obligation to the employees as humans with the potential for growth and improvement, since companies are made up of humans needing to feed families? The parable does not resolve the paradox. Rather, the issues are raised and hearers are left to choose sides.

Paradoxes are valuable because they can raise issues without taking sides. They allow hearers to struggle with a problem that may have no apparent solution. Jesus was famous for using paradox in teaching: "So the last will be first and the first will be last" (Matt 20:16); "Whoever wants to be first must be last of all and servant of all" (Mark 9:35); "For those who want to save their life will lose it, and those who lose their life for my sake, and for the sake of the gospel, will save it" (Mark 8:35); "For all who exalt themselves will be humbled, and those who humble themselves will be exalted" (Luke 14:11). Each of these paradoxes was the concluding remark to a story, parable, or situation that needed pondering. The paradox accentuated the story, parable, or situation being discussed.

"The Parable of the Inexperienced Applicant" also uses the literary device of slice of life.

Word Play

A Peace of the World

An activist and a soldier were sitting together on an airplane headed for a political hotspot in the Third World. They struck up a conversation as travelers often do and pretty soon the topic of their respective occupations came up.

"I'm a soldier of fortune seeking to carve off a little piece of the world for myself," said the one.

"I guess we are in similar occupations then," said the other, "I too am a soldier fighting the good fight for the peace of the world. Though, I've never been very good at finding peace for myself."

The soldier nodded understandingly. "A personal piece can be hard to find for yourself if you're not willing to have courage, look danger in the eye, and persevere. It's a matter of seizing a piece before someone else gets to it first. The piece that is leftover after all the fighting is done isn't worth having. Only the piece taken off the top is of benefit. Not every piece is the same. So the choice has to be made. How much are you willing to sacrifice for the good piece, the one worth possessing?"

"I never thought of peace as a limited resource before. Maybe you're right. Maybe I need to fight a little harder for the right peace so my people won't have to settle for the leftover peace. A little more courage might show others my resolve to gain this right peace. Then maybe I can find peace for myself too. I've always been so scared and my peace has been so elusive."

"If you don't fight hard, then nobody will know how determined you are to bring a piece back with you to enjoy for yourself. Everyone has to find their own piece. Nobody is going to give it away for free!"

"You're right! I can fight the good fight! I can win the race! The right peace is within my grasp. Thanks for the conversation. You've been most helpful."

"Any time."

Many humorous stories and jokes depend upon word play, puns, homonyms, and multiple definitions of words to make their points. These same techniques can also be used in parables for more noble purposes. In "A Peace of the World," the homonyms *peace* and *piece* are used in such a way that two individuals with completely opposite views on life seem to agree with each other when, in fact, they have just talked past each other. In their brief conversation together, the selfish notion of "getting one's piece of the world" is laid side by side with "the peace of the world" and the metaphorical comparison of these two opposite ideologies provides insight into both. The misunderstanding between the soldier and peace activist provides a comic perspective on a serious subject. The *word play type* encompasses all metaphorical comparisons made on the basis of playing with the meanings of words. Jokes are often derived from the misunderstanding, misuse, or play on the definitions of words. The parable must make a point beyond the simple word play.

"A Peace of the World" also makes use of slice of life and paradox. The paradox is found in the concept of "fighting for peace."

Delayed Identification

Finding the Right Church

"This is the third church we've visited this week! Why can't we just pick one and stay there?" the youngster asked her mother.

"Choosing a church is the most important choice you will make in this life, little one. Choosing the right church will determine whether you will live a life of peace and security, or if you'll die of hunger."

"Teach me what to look for, mother. I want to know how to determine a good church from a bad one."

"Crumbs on the floor of the fellowship hall, toys scattered in the nursery, clothing piled high for distribution to the needy, church school papers with crayon doodling scattered throughout the classrooms. These are the things to look for."

"You mean we want to choose a church with a lazy janitor?"

"No, no, little one. In a good church, the best janitor of all won't be able to keep up with the flurry of activity. That's why we'll never starve in a church like that. Always enough food and shelter, and the janitor is too busy with the routine cleaning to bother with a couple of poor church mice."

The little mouse nodded her head. "Let's go check the fellowship hall and see if they had a church dinner last Sunday!"[5]

In "Finding the Right Church," the two main characters are mice, but hearers don't discover this until the next to the last sentence. At the beginning of the parable, hearers are told the main characters are a mother and her daughter looking for a church. Hearers naturally assume the mother and daughter are humans. The church, after all, is a human institution. The dialogue between the two focuses upon the importance of finding a church where they can experience peace and avoid hunger. Hearers assume the two are discussing spiritual issues since the terms "peace" and "spiritual hunger" are metaphors used within churches to allude to spiritual issues. The surprise, or parabolic twist, in the parable comes when hearers discover that the mice were literally speaking of physical security and physical hunger. Only at the end do hearers discover the two subjects thrown side by side for comparison. Mice looking for physical security find it in the same church where humans are experiencing spiritual fulfillment. This unlikely comparison provides a meaningful insight into the nature of what it means to be a vital Christian church. But the comparison could not be made successfully unless the identity of the main characters was obscured until the end of the parable. "Finding the Right Church" also uses the literary devices of fable and slice of life.

For delayed identification to work, the main characters don't have to be animals. They can be any unexpected person or subject including objects. The key to making this literary device work is to set up the initial scene in a stereotypical way so hearers automatically make assumptions about the main character(s) based upon who would ordinarily be found in this particular scene. Because this style typically needs a stereotypical situation to work, these parables are ideal for shedding new light on traditional or stereotypical roles and situations.

Personification of an Object

Money Talks

Mostly I get to see people at their very worst. Occasionally, I've witnessed great acts of charity and self-sacrifice, but those are the exceptions. For every time I've seen a man give to charity, I've seen a hundred times when he's purchased something selfishly for himself. I've known them all in my time: bankers, millionaires, drug dealers, politicians, and gamblers. I briefly met a shopaholic, but our friendship was short-lived. I've been involved in robberies, prostitution, money laundering, and loan sharking. I've traveled the whole world, and could tell stories, lots of unflattering stories.

I'm supposed to be neutral, just a medium of exchange, but it makes me sick to see people fawn all over me while they neglect the needs of their families. I especially hate it when they squeeze me and kiss me with lipstick! They think I'm their best friend, but it's not really me they like. They just like the power they think they have when they hold me in their hot little hands. If they could only see the truth that I can't buy them love, security, friendship, or peace. The best things in life are free. If I could be anything in the world, I wish I could be a love poem. There's real joy and power in love. Instead, I'm stuck being this lousy one hundred dollar bill!

In the *personification of an object style*, a story is told from the point of view of that object. The object is personified so that it speaks with human interest. In "Money Talks," the main character is a one hundred dollar bill, which makes observations about human behavior based upon its unique position as a medium of exchange. This point of view provides a twist in our own human understanding of what it means to use money for purchases. The best things in human life cannot really be purchased with money. "Money Talks" also makes use of the delayed identification style. However, the identity of the object being personified does not always have to be delayed in order for this style to be effective.

Any object that can provide a unique perspective on an issue frequently taken for granted by others can be made into a parable and provide a transformative moment of insight. Emotions can also be effectively personified in this form: fear, anger, joy, sadness. Body parts can likewise be personified. "Left Out" by Charles Schwartz tells a parabolic story from the point of view of the left (non-dominant) hand.[6] The special case of the object being an animal is classified as *fable style* and will be discussed in chapter 5.

Overexaggeration

"The Parable of the Clean Room" in chapter 2 is an example of the literary device of *overexaggeration*. In this parable, a girl never cleans anything in her house. An issue, lack of house cleaning, is examined in its most extreme form. What would be the consequences of taking this idea of a girl who doesn't like to clean to the point of absurdity? The hearer is left to imagine a house where all the dishes are dirty and piled in the sink. The trash has never been carried out. Clothes are left all over the house. The smell must be unbearable. And then the girl must live with the consequences of such an absurd situation: a nice man doesn't want to date a slob.

In real life there are limits set on almost every situation where the normal person would not go. Overexaggeration allows situations and issues to be explored without any limits at all. "What would happen if..." is a common form used in the overexaggeration style. This style is excellent for exploring where the proper limits should be set for a given situation. Real-life situations can be explored from a completely absurd perspective.

Other examples of overexaggeration are "The Parable of the Man Who Mastered the First Date" in chapter 3 and "The Parable of Hypocrisy" in chapter 8. A related literary device is the opposite of overexaggeration: the trivialization of a subject.

Trivialization or Understatement

A Parable of Martyrdom

Competing soap salesmen were avidly promoting their newest product in a suburb of a large city. Convinced by a particularly persistent salesman to try the other brand, Joe took a sample into his home, tried it, and loved it. Not only did Joe love the new brand of soap, but he started talking to all of his neighbors about its virtues. He talked about it so much that his neighbors got tired of hearing about soap. They had made up their own minds about which product they would use and refused to even consider changing. Joe believed in the soap so much that he gave all of his neighbors free samples of the soap, just as the original salesman had given to him. Few of the neighbors tried the sample. Some put it on a shelf. Others threw it in the garbage. But one or two tried the sample, liked the new soap, and changed. When the neighbors who changed told their respective salesmen that they had decided to switch brands of soap, the salesmen became angry. They didn't think it was right for just an average consumer to push a product on their customers. So one night they broke into Joe's home and killed him. To make a statement to Joe's neighbors, they poured Joe's brand of soap all over Joe's dead body. Surprisingly, instead of discouraging the neighbors from changing brands, in sympathy for Joe and out of curiosity about why Joe would be willing to die over a brand of soap, they all tried the free sample he had left them. Most of them liked the new brand of soap and immediately changed. What Joe couldn't get his neighbors to do through his salesmanship, he managed to do through his death.

In "A Parable of Martyrdom," the brand of soap people use becomes so important that Joe is killed for encouraging people to switch brands. Let's be honest: Nobody puts his life on the line for a brand of soap. It just isn't worth dying for. In this parable the issue of soap preferences is trivialized to the point of absurdity. But, precisely because the example is absurd, hearers begin to think about what issues are worth dying for. The example of soap is laid side by side with other subjects until hearers can make sense of what they would be willing to die for. Because the example is understated and Joe is willing to die for a brand of soap, what then would the hearer be willing to die for?

Because *trivialization* is just the opposite of overexaggeration, many of the same principles apply. In trivialization, the use of a very common example that virtually everyone in that particular audience can understand is often an effective subject. The parabolic twist or surprise occurs in the absurdity and triviality of that subject.

Role Reversal

The Graffiti Artists

The boys came back from lunch and found their painting project marred by the destructive work of "taggers" who had spray painted the wall they had been working on all morning.

The first boy sat down on a paint can and remarked, "It isn't even good graffiti! They could have at least used more than one color."

The second boy kicked a rock in disgust.

The supervisor returned a few moments later and just laughed. "Well, it looks like you boys will be putting in a little overtime on this project. Go ahead and get to work. Get that graffiti cleaned up."

The second boy replied, "We already painted that wall. Why should we have to do it again?"

"Yeah," the first boy chipped in, "it's not our fault it got tagged."

The supervisor laughed again. "Both of you will continue to paint this wall until all the graffiti is cleaned up. If you have to paint it fifty times, then that's the way it will have to be." He started to walk off, but the boys stopped him.

"We already painted it once. You saw it! We're not going to do any more work. We're done!"

The supervisor shrugged. "Do what you want, but the judge won't be by to inspect your work until next week. If he thinks you didn't do the work, you know the consequences."

The second boy protested, "But, what happens if the taggers spray paint it again?"

"Simple. You will repaint this wall every day if necessary until the judge gives it the final inspection."

"But, we'll have to set a round-the-clock guard to keep the kids from tagging it!"

"Then you'll have to set a guard. It's no skin off my nose one way or the other. I'm just supposed to see that you have enough paint to do the job."

The boys were silent for a few moments. Then the first boy said, "I'm never going to tag another wall or building ever again."

The supervisor nodded. "I think that's what the judge had in mind when he assigned you this particular community service project to atone for your crimes."

In *role reversal style,* the main characters in the parable act opposite to their stereotype, or they are forced to reverse roles with their opposite, or they are made to experience life from a completely different perspective. In "The Graffiti Artists," two boys who had been caught spray painting (tagging) a wall were assigned community service to clean up that wall. When the wall was tagged in the middle of their repainting, they experienced the anger and frustration of having to clean up somebody else's mess. They felt the same pain their own vandalism caused others. The taggers became frustrated painters. Their roles were reversed.

"The Graffiti Artists" also uses slice of life and delayed identification styles.

Role reversal is an excellent technique for helping people see a different or opposite point of view. This style facilitates understanding and insight into the actions and attitudes of others.

The Form Itself Is the Message

The Parable of Allan's Acronym

Allan had a memory problem. Could he really have so much trouble with names, mathematical formulas, dates, and faces that he couldn't recall them to his conscious mind when he wanted? Remember, certain facts are hard for some people to recollect without help of some kind. Only with mnemonic aids are they able to recall their thoughts in an ordered way. Notes put in a clever format are easier to remember. Yelled, yelped, yawped, it didn't matter how loud Alan said the mnemonic as long as he could associate the memory device with the thing he was supposed to remember. Mnemonically, Allan liked acronyms the very best of all. Therefore, Allan could remember only notes yelled mnemonically with an acronym.

If you found "The Parable of Allan's Acronym" to be an awkward story, you probably didn't get the hidden message. Go back and underline the first word in each sentence (except the last). Then, circle the first letter in each of those words. Now do you get it? The form of the parable is itself the message to be conveyed.

The form is the message style of parable is an excellent vehicle for illustrating structural literary concepts that can be difficult to explain without an illustration. They allow hearers to experience the form instead of being told about it. Marvin Cohen's "The Saving of Surrealism" is another example. Watching a baseball game, the protagonist of the parable bemoans the fact that surrealism is dying while all the poets are taking the afternoon off to watch the game. So, as the game progresses, he finds ways to feed surrealism so it won't die of mass criminal neglect. In the end, his favorite team won the ball game and surrealism survived another day. The entire parable unfolded in a surrealistic form so that the hidden message was that in reading the parable the reader experienced surrealism thereby saving surrealism as an art form. Anyone who didn't understand surrealism before did so afterwards. And, the title of the parable, "The Saving of Surrealism" signaled the hidden message to come.[7]

Especially with beginners inexperienced in the form to be illustrated, clues should be dropped so hearers pay attention to the form. Normally, an author wants the form to remain hidden in the background, so few people pay attention to the form of a literary piece except when the form distracts from the story itself. This is not the case with the form is the message. The form should be highlighted, while the message remains clear.

Allusion to Another Literary Work

The Parable of the Road Not Taken

Two roads diverged before me and sorry I was I could not travel both. I looked down one as far as I could see. Fair it was with promises of a successful career, earthly pleasure, and wealth. Compromises would have to be made to traverse that way. Ethics would not be welcome on this road, no bothersome conscience to divert the traveler from the destination. The poor would be trampled as I climbed the long hill of success on this journey, but the view from the top would be magnificent. The world would be mine to command.

I took the other path just the same, its grassy length wanted wear. The travel would be harder, the path narrower, and the terrain more rugged. There would be fewer oases with which to refresh myself. But, there would be peace on this path, and a free conscience, and a chance to encounter God. Compassion and love would accompany me on this trip and provide moments of joy. The earthly riches would be few, but spiritual riches would be abundant.

Standing at the crossroad, I doubted if I should ever come this way again and have to make so difficult a choice. I shall be telling this with a sigh somewhere ages and ages hence. Two roads diverged in my life, and I took the one less traveled by, and that has made all the difference.

"The Parable of the Road Not Taken" stands on its own with its own message, but its real power comes when hearers recognize the allusion to Robert Frost's famous poem, "The Road Not Taken." The parable intentionally alludes to the poem by using a few key words and phrases in common, particularly from the opening and closing lines. Frost's title is also incorporated in the parable's title as an additional marker for hearer identification. In case the reader is unfamiliar with the poem, here is the original for comparison:

THE ROAD NOT TAKEN

Two roads diverged in a yellow wood,
And sorry I could not travel both
And be one traveler, long I stood
And looked down one as far as I could
To where it bent in the undergrowth;

Then took the other, as just as fair,
And having perhaps the better claim,
Because it was grassy and wanted wear;
Though as for that, the passing there
Had worn them really about the same,

And both that morning equally lay
In leaves no step had trodden black.
Oh, I kept the first for another day!
Yet knowing how way leads on to way,
I doubted if I should ever come back.

I shall be telling this with a sigh
Somewhere ages and ages hence:
Two roads diverged in a wood, and I—
I took the one less traveled by,
And that has made all the difference.[8]

The allusion makes the message of the parable more powerful. However, despite the metaphorical comparison of the poem with the parable, the works are different. The parable does not imitate Frost's poetic form in either rhythm or rhyme. Rather, the parable is true to its own parabolic form using narrative form.

The message delivered by each is also similar, which aids in the metaphorical comparison of the two. In Frost's poem two equally good physical paths are compared. The path less traveled by provided meaning to the poet because it allowed him to be himself without feeling any pressure from the majority who took the other path. He means nothing derogatory about the first path. The first path is a perfectly acceptable way to get to one's destination, and he would have taken that path without reservation if he had not been offered the choice. But, the poem also implies that it is good to choose a less traveled road when the hearer is faced with choosing between equally good metaphysical paths.

In the parable, two metaphysical paths are compared. The metaphysical path less traveled by is the decision to lead a life of physical and spiritual integrity, while the first metaphysical path is the decision to live a life of selfishness at the expense of others. The parable implies the paths are not equally good, and only the second, less traveled, path is worthy of traversing. That does not mean the choice to travel the second path comes easily. That choice comes with regret. The powerful insight provided through the allusion to Frost's poem is that travelers can have genuine regret that they cannot take both paths, even knowing that the second path is truly better.

For *allusion to another literary work* to be effective, hearers must have enough clues to associate the parable with the literary work to which it alludes. In some cases, the parable will be completely ineffective without knowledge of the original work, but without that recognition sometimes a blunted message might come through. The literary work can be a play, novel, poem, hymn, movie, or any clearly recognized famous story. Normally, the allusion should evoke the meaning of the original work. Parables using this style are usually serious so that satire would ordinarily be excluded.

"The Parable of the Road Not Taken" incorporates several direct quotes from Frost's poem. Since I have incorporated 63 words from his 144-word poem, some might argue that quoting 44 percent of the poem goes beyond "fair use." The parable might be considered a "derivative work" for the purposes of copyright law. However, the law is intentionally vague. How much of a work can be quoted as fair use is not defined. When in doubt, permission should be granted from the copyright holder of the original work before publishing any piece that could arguably be defined as a "derivative work." The situation becomes even more complex for third parties who want to use a derivative work someplace else. Third parties must secure permission from *both* the original copyright holder and the copyright holder of the derivative work in order to use a derivative work. This problem is more common when quoting from very short pieces. With novels or longer literary works, fair use normally permits quoting a few lines without legal ramifications as long as it is clear the parable's author intended to allude to the original rather than plagiarize from it. When in doubt, an intellectual-property attorney should be consulted.

Concluding Proverb or the Punch Line Is the Point

The Parable of the Only Volunteer

A local food pantry needed someone to serve as treasurer. The position was voluntary with no salary, but then the task only required a couple of hours of work each week. The bank president turned down the position. He was too important to do such a task. The CEO of the town's factory was too busy. The physician didn't want to. The high school principal declined the job.

The preacher was too busy saving souls. After many weeks of searching, they hadn't found anyone to be treasurer of the food pantry. Everyone turned them down. The position had to be filled, so they gave it to a convicted embezzler who had just been paroled from prison.

Naturally, the story had an unhappy ending. The treasurer left town suddenly, and the food pantry was broke. As for the bank president, CEO, principal, and preacher, they just pointed fingers at each other in anger.

Therefore, volunteer when asked to serve, lest the job be given to someone unqualified.

In "The Parable of the Only Volunteer," the story is simply an illustration of the concluding proverb. The parable can stand alone without the proverb. The *concluding proverb style* takes any guess work out of what conclusion hearers should draw from the parable. By providing the moral, there is no ambiguity about the main point. Teachers can use this style to drive home a point. The story is the prelude that illustrates the proverb. All of the emphasis, and consequently the power, is placed on the concluding proverb. Many fables use this style because fables are often meant for children. As a teaching device, the story makes the proverb easier to remember.

However, the disadvantage of this style is that it excludes other possible interpretations. Hearers are less likely to search for alternative meanings because the moral of the parable has been made crystal clear. The concluding proverb style also short circuits the metaphorical process by allowing hearers to "get" the answer without really working for it.

Any parable can be converted into concluding proverb style format by adding a moralizing conclusion. This may not always be desirable, depending upon the parable teller's intentions and the context in which the parable will be used. However, this style is frequently seen in collections of parables where every parable has a concluding proverb. One can safely assume that most of those proverbs were added by an editor and may not have been intended by the parable's original author. In collections, readers should feel free to search for alternative meanings and not be confined by concluding proverbs.

The fifteenth style, *the fable*, will be explored in chapter 5.

The Two Crabs

One fine day two crabs came out from their home to take a stroll on the sand. "Child," said the mother, "you are walking very ungracefully. You should accustom yourself, to walking straight forward without twisting from side to side."

"Pray, mother," said the young one, "do but set the example yourself, and I will follow you."   Aesop[1]

5.

THE FABLE: NOT JUST FOR CHILDREN

Squirrel Citizenship

One day the squirrels got together to talk about their future in the woods. One squirrel said, "The foxes are eating us up one by one. As long as we live and work separately, the foxes can pick us off individually. We should band together and protect ourselves. As individual squirrels, we are helpless against the foxes, but united we can bravely drive them out of the forest. Also, we can build a squirrel city, like the humans have done, with tree highways and retirement homes and hospitals for sick squirrels." The other squirrels cheered, "Hear, hear! Let's build a squirrel city!" And so they did.

However, a few squirrels hadn't gone to the meeting. They didn't understand the benefits of living in a squirrel city, and they complained about all the new things. Eventually, they enjoyed the squirrel treeways to get around in the woods. They used the squirrel hospital, and they liked the safe deposit boxes at the squirrel banks so they could remember where they hid their stash of acorns.

There was one cranky squirrel nicknamed "Grouch" because he was grouchy all the time. Grouch came to enjoy the benefits of living in the squirrel city too, but he was very unhappy about the cost of participating. The tree in which Grouch's nest was built was in a prime location in the squirrel city, and the squirrel council decided that his tree was the best place to build the new squirrel retirement home because it was a big tree and was next to the squirrel hospital and the squirrel restaurant. Grouch complained, "It's not fair to move my nest to another tree. This tree is mine! My great-grandfather built his first nest in this tree. Go find somewhere else to build your squirrel retirement home." The squirrel council told Grouch, "Since we are a community of squirrels, we must do what is best for all squirrels. Everyone must be a good citizen. We can't think of ourselves only, but must think of what is good for all. Sacrifices have to be made for the good of the community." The squirrel council helped Grouch build a new nest in the squirrel suburbs.

On April 15, the squirrel council came around and took twenty percent of Grouch's acorns for taxes. He complained, "These are my acorns. I found them fair and square. It isn't right for you to take my stuff." Again, the squirrel council told Grouch, "Be a good citizen. We can't think of ourselves only, but must think of what is good for all. Sacrifices have to be made for the good of the community. We are going to use these taxes to build a community center so squirrel children will have a safe place to play."

When the foxes started getting braver and eating young squirrels at the edge of the squirrel city, the squirrel council raised an army to drive the foxes out of the woods altogether. Grouch was too old to go, but they drafted Grouch's grandson to serve in the army. Again, Grouch complained, "My grandson might get hurt. You can't choose him. Choose somebody else." Once again the squirrel council told him, "Be a good citizen. We can't think of ourselves only, but must think of what is good for all. Sacrifices have to be made for the good of the community. With this army we can drive the foxes out of the woods so they won't endanger any squirrels." And the squirrel army did just that. The foxes moved to a different forest and learned to eat rabbits and mice.

One day Grouch hurt his paw on a sharp stick as he traveled the squirrel treeway to visit his son. Grouch complained to the squirrel council, "You need to fix the sharp places in the treeway. I got hurt." The squirrel council told him once again, "Be a good citizen. We can't think of ourselves only, but must think of what is good for all. Sacrifices have to be made for the good of the community. We don't have enough acorns to fix the sharp places on your part of the treeway and still finish the new section of treeway out to the edge of the forest. With the new treeway completed we will be able to import exotic acorns for everyone to enjoy. Next year we will fix the sharp places on your part of the treeway. We have to consider the needs of the majority of squirrels. Be patient, Grouch."

Grouch complained so much because he was selfish. He didn't want to be a good citizen. He wanted only what was best for Grouch. A good citizen understands that sacrifices have to be made for the good of the whole community. We can't think of ourselves only, but must think of what is good for all. And the squirrel community lived happily ever after, except for Grouch. Grouch remained as grouchy as ever.

Since the fable has been the most prevalent literary technique for delivering parabolic instruction through the centuries, it deserves its own special chapter. Aesop and Buddha used fables as far back as the sixth and fifth centuries BCE, making the fable one of the oldest forms of parable. While the parable is generally a story that is plausible, the fable enters the world of fantasy. The normal rules of physics and biology are suspended to deliver a covertly packaged message. In the fable, the main characters are animals, vegetables, or minerals, and they speak and act with human interest and passion. But the general purpose of the fable and the parable are the same, to illustrate moral and spiritual truths by comparison.[2] The fable enables animals or plants to speak plainly about a difficult situation when plain speaking by human counterparts would be offensive. A fantasy story sends the moral to a safe distance from reality so hearers can understand a message that is close to home.[3] The directness of the fable's message is softened because the characters aren't human.

Even though the normal rules of physics and biology can be suspended in a fable, there are still rules the fable must follow. General characterizations about animals as held by the hearers' culture should be observed. For Americans the eagle is a noble bird symbolizing freedom and patriotism. A fable that characterizes the eagle as cowardly or cruel would be offensive to Americans regardless of the intended moral (unless the moral was intended to disparage America or Americans). Likewise, because cattle are sacred to Hindus, cattle should not be portrayed as stupid, gullible, and only valuable as human food when Hindus are the target audience. Beyond cultural issues, the distinctive characteristics of each animal should be respected. Foxes are crafty. Rabbits are fast. Lions are noble. Skunks are smelly. Fish live in water. Birds fly. While children are able to use their imagination vividly, there are limits. Flying snakes and mice the size of houses become ridiculous and distract from the intended moral. Again, exceptions are always permitted, but the fabulist had better have a legitimate reason for deviating from the animal's normal characterizations in order for the fable to be effective. Fables also lose their power when they deviate too much from the hearers' familiarity with an animal's characteristics. While a cobra might be an excellent choice to portray a crafty, dangerous character, North American children would relate better to a rattlesnake. For Indian children the reverse would be true. One of Aesop's fables illustrates these points.

The Dove and the Ant

An Ant, going to a river to drink, fell in, and was carried along in the stream. A Dove pitied her condition, and threw into the river a small bough, by means of which the Ant gained the shore. The Ant afterward, seeing a man with a fowling-piece aiming at the Dove, stung him in the foot sharply, and made him miss his aim, and so saved the Dove's life.

Moral: "Little friends may prove great friends."[4]

The ant is small and weak but a hard worker and loyal to his fellows. Even with these noble characteristics, nobody would expect the ant to save the larger dove. Yet, the ant tries hard and does save the day. The dove, as a symbol of peace, acts in a compassionate and caring manner. Both creatures are portrayed according to their natural and cultural characteristics. The fable works because the hearer is familiar with both the ant and dove and can relate to the ways they interact in the story.

The Advantage of Using Fables with Adults

In "Squirrel Citizenship," the Grouch is constantly complaining about what the community takes from him. But he takes for granted the benefits he gains from being part of the community. He is a grouch because he spends his energy being resentful of his duty to the community without being grateful for the benefits he receives. This fable could easily be translated into a parable by changing all of the squirrel characters into humans. However, the resulting parable becomes more direct and thus more harsh. Everyone knows someone like Grouch, who votes against every school bond proposal and complains about taxes without one shred of gratitude for being able to have fire protection, paved streets, and security from invading armies. A real-life human Grouch would more than likely be offended by the same parable with human characters and understand it as a direct attack upon his character and citizenship. By making the same point indirectly with squirrels acting with human interests, a grouch is less likely to feel directly singled out for a remedial civics lesson. The point is still delivered, but the message has been sugarcoated for easier digestion.

"Squirrel citizenship" is an example of how fables impact adults. In fact, the person most associated with popularizing the fable was also famous for using fables to solve adult conflicts. As an ambassador of the King of Lydia in the sixth century BCE, Aesop used fables to arbitrate disputes and settle delicate affairs of state. He is known to have traveled to Corinth and Athens on state business. But, fables, like parables, are not "magic bullets" that work every time. On his last diplomatic mission, to the city of Delphi, Aesop so insulted the residents that, even though he was a visiting dignitary, he was executed as a common criminal by being pushed off a cliff.

Another historic example of a fable being used in a prophetic way to rebuke adults is Jotham's fable found in the Hebrew Bible. In the twelfth century BCE, the city of Shechem appointed Abimelech as their king after Abimelech had slaughtered seventy of his own brothers. The one surviving brother, Jotham, climbed up on a hill overlooking the coronation site and spoke the following fable to the gathered townspeople:

> The trees once went out to anoint a king over themselves. So they said to the olive tree, "Reign over us." The olive tree answered them, "Shall I stop producing my rich oil by which gods and mortals are honored, and go to sway over the trees?" Then the trees said to the fig tree, "You come and reign over us." But the fig tree answered them, "Shall I stop producing my sweetness and my delicious fruit, and go to sway over the trees?" Then the trees said to the vine, "You come and reign over us." But the vine said to them, "Shall I stop producing my wine that cheers gods and mortals, and go to sway over the trees?" So all the trees said to the bramble, "You come and reign over us." And the bramble said to the trees, "If in good faith you are anointing me king over you, then come and take refuge in my shade; but if not, let fire come out of the bramble and devour the cedars of Lebanon." (Judg 9:8–15)

By implication Jotham was comparing his brother, Abimelech, to the most worthless of all trees. Since the townspeople had selected the most worthless person to rule over them, then they would be destroyed by his bad leadership. Ironically, three years later, Abimelech had a falling out with the city elders and turned his army on the people of Shechem. He laid piles of brush and bramble against the town's tower and set it on fire. A thousand men and women died in the blaze. Just as they had chosen bramble to rule over them, so they were burned up with bramble in the end. Jotham's fable was not only a teaching device to expose the townspeople's stupidity, but became a prophetic object lesson in judgment.

Buddha frequently used fables when teaching adults. Within Buddhist parabolic literature is a specific genre of story called *jataka*, which is the Pali word meaning "birth stories." *Jataka* have their origin with Siddhartha Guatama, the historic Buddha, and are tales about his previous lives while he was on the path to becoming Buddha. In the *Book of the Buddha's Previous Existences,* or *Jataka Book,* 547 of the stories of his previous lives have been collected together. Buddhists generally accept the *jataka* as being likely, if not literally true, and hold the stories as sacred for teaching and inspiration. Many of the *jataka* can be classified as fables, since Buddha was frequently an animal in previous lives.

A typical *jataka* will have four distinct parts. First, Buddha observes a real-life problem. Second, Buddha tells a story about one of his previous existences. Third, the meaning of the *jataka* is explained and Buddha shows how the *jataka* sheds insight on the presenting problem. Fourth, a concluding moral is stated.[5] In the study of parables, *jataka* are fascinating precisely because the original contexts of the stories have been preserved.

Because the *jataka* stories are very old, some of them have been borrowed, modified, and used in Western literature. "Vedabbha and the Thieves," was borrowed by Geoffrey Chaucer to become "The Pardoner's Tale" in his literary classic, *The Canterbury Tales.* "Buddhist Henny-Penny" became the children's story, "Chicken Little." The brothers Grimm rewrote nearly a dozen *jataka* when publishing their famous book of fairy tales, and the Arabian classic, *The Thousand and One Nights,* contains modified versions of *jataka* as well. Nearly a dozen other fables from Tibetan, English, Ethiopian, and Burmese literature were also borrowed from the *jataka.*

Here is a typical example from *Jataka Book.*

Partridge, Monkey, and Elephant

On a certain occasion the Teacher admonished a company of monks to show proper respect for their elders. He related the following story of the past:

In times past, on a slope of Himavat, near a certain huge banyan tree, lived three friends: a partridge, a monkey, and an elephant. They were without respect or deference for each other, having no common life. And to them occurred the following thought: "It is not proper for us to live thus. Suppose we were to live hereafter offering respectful greetings and the other marks of courtesy to that one of us who is the oldest!" "But which one of us is the oldest?" they considered. "This is the way!" said the three animals one day as they sat at the foot of the banyan tree. So the partridge and the monkey asked the elephant: "Master elephant, since how long have you known this banyan tree?" He said: "Friends, when I was a young elephant, I used to go with this banyan sapling between my thighs. Moreover, when I stood with the tree between my thighs, the tips of its branches used to rub against my navel. Thus I have known this tree from the time it was a sapling."

Next the other two animals, in the same way as before, asked the monkey. He said: "Friends, when I was a young monkey, I used to sit on the earth, extend my neck, and eat the tips of the shoots of this banyan tree. Thus I have known it since it was very small."

Finally the other two animals, in the same way as before, asked the partridge. He said: "Friends, in former times, in such-and-such a place, grew a huge banyan tree. I ate its fruits and voided its seed in this place. From that sprang this tree. Thus I know this tree from the time when it had not yet sprouted. Therefore I am older than you." Thus spoke the partridge.

Thereupon the monkey and the elephant said to the wise partridge: "Master, you are older than we. Henceforth to you will we offer respect, reverence, veneration, salutation, and honor; to you will we offer respectful greeting, rising on meeting, homage with joined hands, and proper courtesy; in your admonitions will we abide steadfast. From this time forth, therefore, be good enough to give us admonition and needed instruction."

From that time forth the partridge gave them admonition, established them in the Precepts, and himself also took upon himself the Precepts. And those three animals, established in the Precepts, showed respect and deference for each other, and had a common life. When their life was come to an end, they attained the goal of a heavenly world. The taking upon themselves by these three animals of the Precepts was called the Holy Life of the Partridge.

"For, monks, those animals lived in respectful deference for each other. Why is it that you, who have retired from the world under a Doctrine and Discipline so well taught, do not live in respect and deference for each other?"

When the Teacher had thus related this parable, he assumed the prerogative of One Supremely Enlightened and uttered the following stanza:

Men versed in the Law who honor the aged
Have praise even in this life
And in the next life are in bliss.

When the Teacher had thus extolled the practice of honoring the oldest, he joined the connection and identified the personages in the Birth-story as follows: "At that time the elephant was Moggallana, the monkey was Sariputta, but the wise partridge was I myself."[6]

The four elements of this *jataka* are easily discerned. The presenting problem is monks who do not show proper respect for their elders. The fable of the "Partridge, Monkey, and Elephant" is the stand-alone story. Buddha used the fable to shame the monks into reevaluating how they treated their elders. And the concluding moral is found in the verse extolling the wisdom of those who honor the aged.

As a fable, the *jataka*, "Partridge, Monkey, and Elephant" accomplished its purpose of transforming the behavior of misbehaving monks. Typical of fables, the events described are not plausible, but that has not stopped Buddhists from finding great wisdom in this fable anyway. Huge banyan trees like the one described in the fable are one hundred years in the growing. The likelihood of any one of the three animals being that old is remote: Asian elephants have a life span of seventy to eighty years, monkeys native to India have a life span of about twenty years, and gray partridges live less than eight years. For the partridge to be the oldest, the monkey, elephant, and banyan tree would have had to be less than eight years old. But the fable is still true to the nature of each character and this is what saves the story. The banyan tree is revered and respected. The animals take pride in recounting their memories of the tree as it grows. The partridge eats the fig of the banyan tree and the seeds go straight through the bird's digestive system unaffected. The elephant and monkey are both portrayed as honorable and trustworthy. Buddhists have tended not to be concerned about the plausibility of Buddha's *jataka*. Like the fable, the *jataka* derives its power not from its plausibility, but by its ability to deliver a moral.

In the case of Aesop and Buddha, many of their original fables or *jataka* were spoken to adults. Generations that followed recycled those fables, adding concluding proverbs and using them to teach moral lessons to small children. For many centuries the use of fables has been so associated with children's stories that serious preachers, speakers, and writers have been reluctant to use this genre with adults. "That's kid's stuff," is a common way fables are dismissed by both adult speakers and hearers. However, fables can be particularly effective with adults when used in a way that does not make them feel like children.

In days gone by, fables were a staple of most children's literature. This is not the case anymore. A whole plethora of new children's literature has been written in the last few decades so that many children and young adults are no longer familiar with Aesop's fables and Grimm's fairy tales. With younger adult audiences, fables do not have the "kid's stuff" stigma as they do with older audiences who were force-fed Aesop as a toddler. Preachers and teachers should feel free to occasionally incorporate a fable or two in their sermons and lectures. Fables can be used in any venue in which a parable can be used. I suggest not making a great deal about introducing a fable as such. Rather, introduce it as a story. Adults like stories too. They just don't like admitting it, and they don't want to feel preached down to or childish in the process. Also, avoid using any concluding proverb associated with the fable. Let the story itself work parabolically. In many cases, reading the concluding proverb following the fable provokes the same groan as finally hearing the punch line of a dumb joke. Fables have a long history for use with adults, and there isn't any reason they shouldn't continue to be used with adults.

The Advantage of Using Fables with Children

The long association fables have with children's literature already testifies to their value in providing moral education to children. Fables can be used as children's sermons in worship, moral lessons in a camp or group setting, and nightly bedtime stories. They are great for use in traveling because fables are short and don't require children to look at pictures. The imagery within the fable creates its own pictures within the child's mind. As children get older, they can read fable collections for themselves. As mentioned before, fables are, for the most part, currently out of fashion in children's literature. Many adults were force-fed Aesop as a child and are looking for something different for their own children. Since adults are the primary purchaser of children's books, the market caters as much to what adults *think* children will like as it does to the children's tastes themselves. Children don't have prejudices about how ancient fables were used with their parents' and grandparents' generations. Children simply like stories. Fables are suitable stories for children because they are short, inspire curiosity, and make great discussion starters.

Fables can be read to children individually or in a group context. When reading to a child individually, the reader should pause between fables and let the child talk about the story. Let the child ask questions and make observations. Refrain from reading any concluding proverb until the child has exhausted her comments. The child may see other possibilities within the story that fascinate her. Sometimes the child will make comments that seem strange or offtrack. Don't be afraid to gently probe what she means or how that relates to the fable. Never scold a child for making a tangential or unrelated point. Rebukes discourage discussion and will prevent her from taking risks by making comments in the future. When the child is entirely offtrack, gently steer the conversation back to the fable. Encourage a shy child by asking direct and easy questions. Only after all the discussion has been completely explored should any concluding proverb be read. The reader can even ask the child if the concluding proverb is relevant to the fable. If time permits, move on to the next fable.

When used with groups of children, the same principles apply. Encourage discussion and let the children make their points before offering an opinion on the fable's meaning. Don't let any single child monopolize the discussion. Ask shy children very simple and direct questions about the story to encourage their participation. Compliment their participation so they know that their views are valued. Children have a special gift for discerning sincerity in adults. Genuinely be with them in the process of reading and discussing the fable. After the event is over, the reader can worry about whether other adults overhearing the discussion were impressed. At the time of the fable telling, become absorbed in the children's presence. After all, the event is about the children, not the fabulist.

When fables are used as a children's sermon in worship, the reader should make an attempt to find a fable that delivers a moral that complements the scripture passages for the day and meshes well with the preacher's message to the adults. If a particular fable cannot be found, write one! Or, adapt an existing fable for use with the theme of that particular worship service. Fables lend themselves for use with mixed audiences of children and adults. Adults will enjoy the fable as much as the children.

Even though fables work well with mixed audiences, fabulists should be aware that the meaning drawn from the fable will likely be a little different for children than for adults. There are developmental differences between adults and children that cause moral lessons to be processed differently. Children are concrete thinkers and are more prone to understand a story literally. They are able to use their imagination more readily and immerse themselves in the literalness of the fable: squirrels *do* build squirrel cities and ants *do* care what happens to doves! While children are less concerned about a story's plausibility, they also might need a little prompting to find the fabulist's intended moral. I would still let the children discuss the fable and its implications before guiding them to the intended moral, but the fabulist should not be afraid to actually guide the discussion and help shape their conclusions. With children, using a concluding proverb or explaining the moral helps the children associate the story with the intended moral. This makes the moral more memorable, and as their developmental processes mature provides a metaphorical story with which to continually compare the moral.

The fable also has the advantage of being an indirect teaching method. When an adult tries to teach a child, there is a disparity of power between the two and the child must accept the adult's authority in order for the lesson to be absorbed. However, when a fable is told, the adult speaker leaves the role of teacher and becomes a storyteller. The characters in the fable teach the moral. In the case of "Squirrel Citizenship" it is the squirrel council who delivers the moral, "Everyone must be a good citizen. We can't think of ourselves only, but must think of what is good for all. Sacrifices have to be made for the good of the community." All authority issues between the adult teacher and the children students are moved to the background as the squirrels become the teachers of good citizenship. The adult teacher can repeat the fable's moral, but only after the children have drawn it out first. This principle is likewise important in the use of parables. The seventeenth-century Islamic dervish, Amil-Baba, refused to take credit for any of the parables he told so that "nobody stands between the learner and that which is learned."[7]

While using fables to teach moral lessons should be encouraged for small children, not every fable teaches a lesson that is appropriate or relevant in the twenty-first century. Care should be taken to select fables that edify. Culture has changed a great deal since Aesop wrote his fables and not all of Aesop's fables teach lessons we would want twenty-first-century children to emulate. Take for instance Aesop's "The Farmer and the Cranes."

The Farmer and the Cranes

Some cranes made their feeding grounds on plowlands newly sown with wheat. For a long time the farmer, brandishing an empty sling, chased them away by the terror he inspired; but when the birds found that the sling was only swung in the air, they ceased to take any notice of it and would not move. The farmer, on seeing this, charged his sling with stones, and killed a great number. The remaining birds at once forsook his fields, crying to each other, "It is time for us to be off to Liliput: for this man is no longer content to scare us, but begins to show us in earnest what he can do."

Concluding Proverb: If words suffice not, blows must follow.[8]

The fable teaches that violence *is* an acceptable way to make a point. While this might have been a socially acceptable way of dealing with conflict in centuries gone by, this is not a moral lesson most religious leaders would want to see taught today. This fable should be skipped when reading fables to children. Or, the creative teacher can modify the ending to provide a more appropriate ending. Try this adapted version of "The Farmer and the Cranes."

The Farmer and the Cranes (Adapted)

Some cranes made their feeding grounds on farmland newly sown with wheat. For a long time the farmer, brandishing an empty sling, chased them away by the terror he inspired; but when the birds realized that the sling was only swung in the air, they ceased to take any notice of it and would not move. The farmer, on seeing this, asked the birds why they were stealing his wheat. The birds replied that they were hungry. They noted that the farmer had plenty of wheat in the field for his own needs and enough extra to sell. The cranes were only interested in eating enough to stave off their hunger. The farmer considered their situation and offered them a deal. The farmer did have an excess amount of grain he could share with the cranes provided they would help him by eating bugs in another field. The cranes found his terms quite acceptable and both the farmer and the cranes were happy with their new situation.

Concluding Proverb: Negotiation works better than threats.

The adapted version leaves readers with a healthier moral lesson for the twenty-first century. The farmer learns to share while the cranes work for their meal by eating bugs. The new moral teaches children that empty threats are not effective in getting one's way. Aesop's fables have long been in the public domain, and adapting them presents no legal difficulties. This may not be the case with other collections of fables and parables. Care should be taken when publishing fables you have adapted from other sources. When in doubt about the copyright issues, contact a lawyer who specializes in intellectual property law.

Whether the reader chooses to adapt an ancient fable or simply skips it when reading a collection to children, the reader must have read the fables in advance. When teaching children, either individually or in a group, they deserve a prepared and competent teacher. Teachers who do not spend time in preparation do great disservice to their students. Even parents reading to their children at home should be careful to screen the literature they read to them. This is also true of television programs and movies. When I go to the theater, I'm horrified to see the number of small children parents have brought to see R-rated movies. Children deserve to have age-appropriate literature and cinema available to them that teaches life lessons they can understand. This necessarily means their adult caretakers and teachers need to be responsible and discriminating in their selection of books and movies.

Mislabeled and Borderline Fables and Parables

Parables and fables are frequently mislabeled in practice. Not all of Buddha's previous lives were as animals, so some of the *jataka* would more precisely be categorized as parable rather than fable. Likewise, not all of Aesop's fables had animals as main characters and are more properly called parables. Aesop wrote both types of literature, although his collection of work is known as fable. No great literary sin has been committed by grouping fables and parables together. The categories are made only for the sake of teaching about them. Either story can be thoroughly enjoyed without knowing its exact label.

Beyond mislabeled stories, there are some stories that defy classification. Between the parable, which is generally a plausible story, and the fable, which is firmly rooted in fantasy, is a more ambiguously defined hybrid story that is neither and both at the same time. Some of the short stories of Enrique Anderson Imbert fall into this category. In "Light Pedro," after a man recovers from a mysterious illness he starts losing weight. He loses so much weight over time that he gradually becomes lighter than air. Pedro continues about his daily life with stones in his pocket to weigh him down. Eventually, Pedro's wife has to tie a cord around his leg to keep him from floating away. In the closing scene, he is sleeping on the ceiling and a puff of wind blows him out the open window and he begins his voyage to infinity.[9] The story is told in such a believable manner that it does not feel like fantasy. Yet, the story really isn't plausible either. Furthermore, any moral that could be derived from the story (and several can be) is not made crystal clear.

The same difficulty is encountered when classifying fables that border upon fairy tale. James Thurber's *The 13 Clocks* reads like a fairy tale, but the plot is so intricately interconnected in a symbolic way as to have parabolic implications.[10] The story has magical creatures, witches, and characters stereotypical of fairy tales. The literary technique of exaggeration is used to make the evil duke particularly sinister and the hero prince to be especially naive. *The 13 Clocks* has several morals that can be drawn from it: good always overcomes evil; destiny is irrefutable; or evil intentions can be used to bring about good. But the story seems to be more metaphorically rich than the average fairy tale. The final classification of fairy tale does not seem to be quite right. While working definitions are useful for teaching and discussing parabolic literature, the lines of demarcation from one form of literature to the other are often fuzzy and blurred. Such is the nature of metaphorical literature.

In the oral tradition of cultural storytelling, stories passed from person to person, generation to generation, as the living, evolving, creative expressions of a people's understanding of themselves and their world. The intention of the storyteller was not the verbatim recitation of some static text. It was to bring alive the underlying truth of a story in a manner appropriate to a particular audience at a particular moment. David C. Korten[1]

6.
PARABLES WORKING IN CONTEXT

The Two Contexts of Life and Literature

The Parable of the Innocent Car Ride?

The receptionist for an accounting firm was always quick to share a juicy tidbit of gossip when she ran across it. During a coffee break, she shared the following true story with Bill, Sandra, and Doug, "As I was unlocking the front door this morning, I saw Mike get out of the boss's new Corvette. And Suzanne's hair was a little messed up! You know what *that* means, don't you?" All three coworkers nodded in assent.

Later that morning, Bill barged into Mike's office and slapped him on the back. "So you're having an affair with the boss I hear. Congratulations! Suzanne's a real looker. I've been lusting after her for years."

Mike escorted Bill from his office saying, "Bill, you're disgusting. Get out."

At lunch, Sandra came up to Mike and said, "Sorry to hear your car broke down again. Do you need a ride home today? I go near your place on my way home. I hope the repair bill won't keep you from going to the game with the crew on Friday night."

Mike looked confused, "What makes you think my car broke down again?"

Sandra smiled in her little impish way and said, "Oh, a little birdie told me." Then, she walked off.

Later that afternoon Doug walked into Mike's office all dejected and slouched down in a chair. "It's not fair that you're getting a promotion and I'm not. I've been with the company longer than you have and I work really hard."

Mike threw up his hands in shock, "How did you possibly come to the conclusion I'm getting a promotion?"

"Mr. Johnson used to take his employees on a long drive when he offered them a promotion. I don't know if it's true or not, but they used to say that anyone who turned down his offer had to walk home. You were seen…"

Mike laughed, "I get it. Everyone saw me get out of Suzanne's car this morning. That's what all this craziness is about!" Mike got up and walked to the door of his office and shouted down the hall, "Look, all you busybodies out there. My car ride with Suzanne this morning was completely innocent and entirely none of your business."

The context in which hearers of a story live shapes their understanding of life and of the story heard. In "The Parable of the Innocent Car Ride?" three people interpreted an incident reported to them in three different ways. All of them jumped to conclusions based upon their own preconceived notions of what it means to get out of a car with the boss early in the morning. The literary device used in this parable is the unfinished tale. Readers are not told what Mike was doing with his boss so early in the morning, so they are forced to supply their own conclusions based upon their own personal contexts like the three coworkers.

Mike and Suzanne could have been coming back from a Rotary breakfast meeting in her Corvette. They could have had an early meeting with a new client, or they might have been plotting to murder Suzanne's ex-husband's girlfriend. There is no "right" answer to what they were doing. Readers are not told. But readers do provide a speculative ending based upon their own experiences. What the author intended by this teaching-metaphor parable was to get readers to think about how events are interpreted.

Every parable lives in two different contexts at the same time: the context in which the story is set, and the context in which hearers of the story live. Each plays an important role in how parables are interpreted. Parables start as stories in the mind of a storyteller. Part of the context in which the story is set is the original intention of its author. What problem did the parable teller observe that prompted her to design a parable to be the solution? The story of the parable must also have a context. The intention of the parable teller and the specific setting of the story make up the original context. Hearers who do not understand the original context of the story may not come to the conclusion the parable teller intended. Take one of Jesus's parables as a case in point.

The Parable of the Pounds

A nobleman went to a distant country to get royal power for himself and then return. He summoned ten of his slaves, and gave them ten pounds, and said to them, "Do business with these until I come back." But the citizens of his country hated him and sent a delegation after him, saying, "We do not want this man to rule over us." When he returned, having received royal power, he ordered these slaves, to whom he had given the money, to be summoned so that he might find out what they had gained by trading. The first came forward and said, "Lord, your pound has made ten more pounds." He said to him, "Well done, good slave! Because you have been trustworthy in a very small thing, take charge of ten cities." Then the second came, saying, "Lord, your pound has made five pounds." He said to him, "And you, rule over five cities." Then the other came, saying, "Lord, here is your pound. I wrapped it up in a piece of cloth, for I was afraid of you, because you are a harsh man; you take what you did not deposit, and reap what you did not sow." He said to him, "I will judge you by your own words, you wicked slave! You knew, did you, that I was a harsh man, taking what I did not deposit and reaping what I did not sow? Why then did you not put my money into the bank? Then when I returned, I could have collected it with interest." He said to the bystanders, "Take the pound from him and give it to the one who has ten pounds." (And they said to him, "Lord, he has ten pounds!") "I tell you, to all those who have, more will be given; but from those who have nothing, even what they have will be taken away. But as for these enemies of mine who did not want me to be king over them—bring them here and slaughter them in my presence." (Luke 19:12–27)

In the first-century Palestinian culture of Jesus's day, valuables were often secured from theft by wrapping them in a piece of cloth and hiding them in the household. Hearers familiar with the culture of that day heard that the slave wrapped his pound up in a piece of cloth and would have nodded their approval. This was a customary practice and considered safe. The twist in the story comes when Jesus condemns the man who had practiced a customary way of protecting valuables. Jesus's original hearers would be shocked because each of them probably had secured valuables in a similar way. The parable condemned them for being appropriately safe and responsible!

A modern reader unfamiliar with first-century practice for securing valuables hears the story and concurs in Jesus's condemnation of the man who wrapped his pound in a piece of cloth. By twenty-first-century standards his practice is considered irresponsible. He should have at least taken the pound to a bank's safety deposit box if he wasn't going to invest it! Twenty-first-century hearers miss the twist and lose part of the intended meaning. *Jesus was condemning those who played it safe.* God expected them to take risks with the talents entrusted to their care, not to be safe.

Likewise, without a knowledge of the history of Palestine, twenty-first-century hearers might not understand the execution part of the story. That dissenters were slaughtered before the king's eyes seems a little harsh for a story about investing wisely! However, this scenario was easily recognizable to first-century hearers. Though the Romans had avoided the title *king* for their own rulers for several centuries, they granted the title at times to certain ethnic rulers in the eastern provinces of the empire. In 40 BCE Herod the Great defeated the Parthians with the aid of Roman troops and was awarded the title *king*. After Herod's death, Archelaus was given half of his father's kingdom. He journeyed to Rome in 4 BCE to have himself declared a king as his father was before him. The title would have given Archelaus more prestige and power in the Roman Empire. However, at the same time, a group of fifty persons were sent by Archelaus's enemies to resist his appointment. Caesar Augustus awarded Archelaus only the title of *ethnarch*. When he got home, Archelaus ruthlessly took out his revenge on those who had opposed him. First-century hearers of Jesus's parable would immediately be reminded of this notorious event. They would understand the importance of maintaining their loyalty to the king.

"The Parable of the Pounds" *does* have meaning for twenty-first-century hearers. However, the meaning they derive from the parable is probably not all that Jesus intended. In the original context, hearers would be shocked to learn that playing it safe is not acceptable to God and loyalty to God must be absolute. In the twenty-first-century context, hearers concur with Jesus that those who hide their money at home are being careless and slothful, which means that people should invest their talents wisely so that they gain a return for God's kingdom. The two interpretations are similar enough to be in the purview of what Jesus probably intended, but those who understand the original context get a sharper message.

When a parable is supplied to a reader without any original context at all, the reader automatically supplies her own context. Take Jesus's parable of "The Lost Coin" as a case in point.

The Lost Coin

> Or what woman having ten silver coins, if she loses one of them, does not light a lamp, sweep the house, and search carefully until she finds it? When she has found it, she calls together her friends and neighbors, saying, "Rejoice with me, for I have found the coin that I had lost." (Luke 15:8–9)

A young girl hearing this parable for the first time might ask, "So why didn't she just ask her dad for another coin?" The girl puts herself in the parable and projects how she would handle the identical situation today. To her, a coin represents only a small unit of money that is always supplied by her father. If she lost a coin, instead of looking diligently for it, she might cry and ask her father to replace it. Small children are often not developmentally able to make a distinction between their own contexts and the contexts of others. All parables will always be interpreted from an individual's point of view. Those using parables need to be aware of the contexts of their audience. If there is a substantial difference between the original context and that of the hearers', then background information will have to be supplied, or the parable teller will have to understand that the parable may not have the original intended effect. When working with children, this principle is easily understood. However, many adults are not able to get outside of their own contexts and understand a parable from someone else's perspective. Parable tellers always have to take into account the difference between the original context and the context of the current hearers even when they are not using their own parables.

Sometimes the original context of a parable is simply unknown. Parables encountered in a collection, for instance, are often given without an original context. Readers ponder the parable, struggle with the twist, but do so strictly with their own personal situations in mind. Even if historical data and cultural background are known about the author, without knowing the circumstances of the parable's source, part of the original context is missing and readers cannot be sure how the parable was supposed to be understood. If readers are primarily interested in the author's original intention, they are left frustrated. If they are looking for insight or personal enrichment, they are unconcerned about the original context and will let the parable speak to them in their own contexts.

Removing parables from their original contexts can give them a timeless quality. Without the burden of their original contexts, parables can have a relevant meaning in every age. Many of Jesus's parables have been interpreted differently through the centuries. Each new generation of biblical scholars is quick to denounce the interpretations of those who have come before them, but that does not mean the original interpretations were not helpful in the age in which they were formulated. A classic example from the Christian tradition is Jesus's "Parable of the Laborers in the Vineyard."

The Parable of the Laborers in the Vineyard

For the kingdom of heaven is like a landowner who went out early in the morning to hire laborers for his vineyard. After agreeing with the laborers for the usual daily wage, he sent them into his vineyard. When he went out about nine o'clock, he saw others standing idle in the marketplace; and he said to them, "You also go into the vineyard, and I will pay you whatever is right." So they went. When he went out again about noon and about three o'clock, he did the same. And about five o'clock he went out and found others standing around; and he said to them, "Why are you standing here idle all day?" They said to him, "Because no one has hired us." He said to them, "You also go into the vineyard." When evening came, the owner of the vineyard said to his manager, "Call the laborers and give them their pay, beginning with the last and then going to the first." When those hired about five o'clock came, each of them received the usual daily wage. Now when the first came, they thought they would receive more; but each of them also received the usual daily wage. And when they received it, they grumbled against the landowner, saying, "These last worked only one hour, and you have made them equal to us who have borne the burden of the day and the scorching heat." But he replied to one of them, "Friend, I am doing you no wrong; did you not agree with me for the usual daily wage? Take what belongs to you and go; I choose to give to this last the same as I give to you. Am I not allowed to do what I choose with what belongs to me? Or are you envious because I am generous?" So the last will be first and the first will be last. (Matt 20:1–16)

In a sermon on this passage from the fifth century, Saint Augustine of Hippo interpreted the parable as follows.

There is also something like this in this present life, and besides that solution of the parable, by which they who were called at the first hour are understood of Abel and the righteous men of his age, and they at the third, of Abraham and the righteous men of his age, and they at the sixth, of Moses and Aaron and the righteous men of their age, and they at the eleventh, as in the end of the world, of all Christians; besides this solution of the parable, the parable may be seen to have an explanation in respect even of this present life. For they are as it were called at the first hour, who begin to be Christians fresh from their mother's womb; boys are called as it were at the third, young men at the sixth, they who are verging toward old age, at the ninth hour, and they who are called as if at the eleventh hour, are they who are altogether decrepit; yet all these are to receive the one and the same denarius of eternal life.

But, Brethren, hearken ye and understand, lest any put off to come into the vineyard, because he is sure, that, come when he will, he shall receive this denarius. And sure indeed he is that the denarius is promised him; but this is no injunction to put off. For did they who were hired into the vineyard, when the householder came out to them to hire whom he might find, at the third hour for instance, and did hire them, did they say to him, "Wait, we are not going thither till the sixth hour"?[2]

Augustine provided multiple possibilities for interpretation of the parable using the allegorical method. This sermon was found to be very instructive in his own age as the church was struggling to understand its identity apart from Judaism. This sermon was collected and saved after his death and has scarcely been out of print since.

Writing in the sixteenth century, John Calvin blasted Augustine's interpretation with these words:

> There are some who give an ingenious interpretation to this passage, as if Christ were distinguishing between Jews and Gentiles. The Jews, they tell us, were called *at the first hour,* with an agreement as to the hire; for the Lord promised to them eternal life, on the condition that they should fulfil the law; while, in calling the Gentiles, no bargain was made, at least as to works, for salvation was freely offered to them in Christ. But all subtleties of that sort are unseasonable; for the Lord makes no distinction in the bargain, but only in the time; because those who entered *last,* and in the evening, *into the vineyard,* receive the same hire with *the first.*[3]

Calvin was writing at the beginning of the Reformation, when people were rediscovering the Bible. Calvin was interested in the *literal* words and their application. His only concern in interpretation was understanding the parable in relation to the stated reason why Jesus told the story, "But many who are first will be last, and the last will be first" (Matt 19:30). Calvin wrote, "As this parable is nothing else than a confirmation of the preceding sentence, the last shall be first, it now remains to see in what manner it ought to be applied."[4] Calvin went on to conclude that those who became Christians earlier should not look down upon people who were converted to Christ later, but should continue their service in humility and love. All Christians will receive the common prize.

Writing in the mid-twentieth century, Joachim Jeremias blasted Calvin's interpretation with these words:

> Against the view that the parable is intended to illustrate the way in which at the Last Day the first will become last and the last first, it is not a valid objection that not merely two, but five groups are concerned, since from v. 8 onward only the first- and last-mentioned groups occupy the stage; the three intermediate groups are forgotten; they were only introduced to illustrate the circumstances leading up to the engagement of labourers, especially the urgent need of workers. But it may be possible to raise another objection to the view that the parable is intended to illustrate the final reversal of order at the Last Day....There can be no great significance in the order of payment; a couple of minutes earlier or later can hardly be said to assign precedence to any one or deprive him of it. In fact, no complaint is made later on about the order of payment which, taken in its context, should merely emphasize the equality of the last with the first....In any case the parable certainly conveys no lesson about the reversal of rank at the end since all receive exactly the same wage.[5]

Jeremias goes on to conclude that the meaning of the parable is about God's generosity. If the laborers hired last had been given only the wage for working one hour, their families would have gone hungry. The vineyard owner was providing a living wage to everyone for the sake of compassion on each worker's family.

In truth, there is nothing inherently wrong with any of these three conclusions to the "Parable of the Laborers in the Vineyard." Augustine, Calvin, and Jeremias all provided theologically insightful comments to their own generation about what this parable could mean. But, rather than admit that the earlier interpretations could have been relevant at the time (but no longer), they simply proclaimed that those interpretations were wrong. Rather, the context of the hearers changed, and so did their interpretations of the parable.

Meister Eckhart developed a parabolic interpretation of scripture that has much to commend it. He taught that scriptures have both a literal meaning and a parabolic meaning. The parabolic meaning is the more hidden sense contained "under the shell of the letter." He argued that more mature readers could find nuances of meaning in scripture beyond the literal meaning intended. Basically, Eckhart understood that differences necessarily arose between the context of the author and the context of the reader. He did not perceive a problem with an interpretation not intended by the original author as long as that interpretation was true. Concerning the parabolic method of interpreting scripture, Eckhart wrote,

> Since the literal sense is that which the author of a writing intends, and God is the author of holy scripture, as has been said, then every true sense is a literal sense. It is well known that every truth comes from the Truth itself; it is contained in it, derived from it and is intended by it....What harm does it do to me that different meanings can be taken from the same words as long as they are true, and true in the single truth of the Light? God, the Truth Himself, the author of scripture, comprehends, inspires and intends all truth at one time in his intellect.[6]

Eckhart was not arguing that every interpretation was true: Some interpretations were false, not because the interpreter wasn't thinking about scripture when the interpretation was made, but because those interpretations were not consistent with the rest of Christian doctrine. However, if a tangential meaning is taken from a passage, and that meaning is consistent with the rest of Christian doctrine, then no harm is done. Eckhart was also quick to say that the parabolic method was not intended for beginners. Beginners should master the literal method of interpreting scripture before moving on to advanced hermeneutics.

Likewise, in the interpretation of any parable, the context in which the hearer lives is going to influence what meaning the hearer takes from it. While there are several valid and tangential meanings that can be true, not every interpretation can be true. The boundary separating valid interpretations from false ones is ambiguous and broad. The diviner of systematic truth walks up to the precipice's edge and looks over. One more step and he falls to his death. The diviner of parabolic truth walks out into the marsh and slowly sinks deeper and deeper into the mire until he drowns. While there are limits to what is an acceptable interpretation to a parable, that limit is much more difficult to pin down than when dealing with simple propositional statements.

Timing Is a Part of Context

As people grow and mature in faith, their personal contexts change. A person will not interpret an event at age fifty as he would have when he was twelve. Also, the culture in which individuals live moves on. Fashions, political ideology, and technology all change. Each moment in an individual's life is merely a single frame in an ever-rolling film. One person might read the same parable at different points in her life and derive three different meanings from it because her context has changed. The Sufi master Halqavi said, "Only a very few Sufi tales can be read by anyone at any time and still affect the 'Inner consciousness' constructively. Almost all others depend upon where, when and how they are studied. Thus most people will find in them only what they expect to find: entertainment, puzzlement, allegory."[7] Therefore, the timing of when a parable is read in a hearer's life is part of that hearer's context.

That the deepest meaning of a parable cannot always be discerned by beginning students is not always a bad thing. Beginners in the faith are enthusiastic and full of joy. The advanced lessons in faith can be quite frightening to a beginner. Loving one's enemies and offering oneself as a sacrifice for the sake of others are difficult lessons that are best learned in sequence. As the student matures in the faith, the deeper meanings of parables seep out and allow the student to continue to grow in faith. When the time is right, when the student is able to hear a deeper message, the student's subconscious will allow that message to come through and provide transformation.

Timing is also part of the parable teller's context. A perfectly crafted judicial parable will fail if the parable is not told when the hearer is able to perceive the hidden message. Care must go into preparing the hearer for the parable. Then, at the right time, the parable is brought out to do its work. An alcoholic might be influenced by a parable, but not while he is drunk. A student might gain insight from a teaching-metaphor parable, but not when she is tired. A man might be searching for an example to imitate, but won't grasp it when he is irritable. Telling the parable at the right time is just as important as the brilliance of the parable itself.

When neurotics come to you for help, they seldom seek to be healed, for healing is painful. What they really want is to be made comfortable in their neuroses. Or, best of all, they yearn for a miracle that will heal them painlessly. Anthony de Mello[1]

7.

PARABLES AND THE UNSYMPATHETIC AUDIENCE

Truth, Lies, and Hypocrisy

The Parable of Hypocrisy

There was a man who took great pride in his ability to keep his house clean. He believed that he had the cleanest house in the whole town. He spent hours and hours each day dusting, vacuuming, and polishing everything in his house. He knew without a shadow of a doubt that he spent more time cleaning than did any other person in the whole city. His was the cleanest house!

One day, the man decided to have an open house so that everyone else could see what a beautiful and clean house he had. As the first group of visitors entered through the front door, the man lit a tiny candle and proceeded to lead them on a tour of the living room, dining room, kitchen and the upstairs bedrooms. Confidently, he boasted of the many long hours he put in cleaning the place every day. Certain that no one would find fault with the immaculate way he kept everything so clean, he even challenged the group to find even the tiniest speck of dust.

One elderly woman, exasperated that she couldn't see anything because the house was so dark, groped her way to a window and pulled back the heavy black curtains which virtually blocked all the sunlight from outside. She said, "Sugar, you can't expect us to see much unless you snuff out that teeny candle and let some real light come in."

Once the sunlight had cut through the stifling darkness, the rest of the group gasped. There were spots here and there which had obviously been polished, but most of the room was filled with such filth that the group was embarrassed for the man. The elderly woman compassionately gave the man a motherly pat on the shoulder and said, "You might spend lots of time cleaning, but it helps if you have some real light so you can see what you're doing. Show me where the cleaning supplies are and we'll help you tidy up a bit before anyone else comes by."

The man looked around the room in disbelief at the dirt and filth. Cradling his tiny candle, he angrily went to the window to see what power had desecrated his spotlessly clean house. Seething with rage, he stared at the bright sun in the sky until he went blind. Then, his anger abated, and his former happiness returned. His house was clean again.[2]

Appearances are more important to some people than the truth. In "The Parable of Hypocrisy," the homeowner was angered that his boasts had been exposed as untrue. Maintaining the appearance of cleanliness was more important to him than whether the house was really clean. Keeping his house in darkness was the method he used to hide the uncleanness from everybody else, and also from himself. While the true seeker would have welcomed the help the elderly woman offered, the hypocrite was angry at the exposure. Furthermore, because the man reacted so angrily to the truth and went blind cursing the light that exposed him, he was worse off from his contact with the truth than he was before the truth was revealed to him.

Truth can be dangerous. The wise dispenser of truth is able

to discern when and how truth can be revealed for benefit as opposed to harm. In "The Parable of Hypocrisy," the man was unable to deal with the reality presented to him. Sometimes the raw truth is so painful or overpowering that its presentation is more harmful than helpful. Precautions should be taken when delivering a truthful but unpopular message to an unsympathetic audience. The truth is not always enough to keep people from harm. This applies to the one who reveals truth as well as to the audience.

If humans were strictly logical creatures, then decisions could be based solely upon the rightness or wrongness of a potential choice. But humans are emotional creatures. How people will react to truth has to be taken into consideration when sharing it. After all, sharing the truth with someone should promote love and health. But when this does not happen, then the dispenser of truth must use discernment regarding how much, if any, of a truth can be revealed to hearers in order to bring about a more healthful outcome.

Not all truth is equal in importance. Truth that applies to character and maturity are more important than truth about superficial things. Truth about superficial things can hurt feelings. A husband's opinion that his wife's new hairstyle is atrocious might hurt her feelings if he shared this truth with her. He might withhold it from her in order to spare her feelings because he values her love and friendship more than his right to share his opinion. Regarding superficial things, like appearances and preferences, truth is subjective. However, in regard to truth about character and maturity, there is less subjectivity. The convicted thief might find it uncomfortable to hear the judge lecture him about his lack of character, but the punishment dispensed is meant to transform him into a more mature citizen. His feelings are less important than the possibility that he will change by being forced to hear the truth about himself. Between these two extreme examples are a whole multitude of possibilities in which the hearer's feelings and potential reactions have to be weighed against the hearer's character development. Sometimes the truth regarding superficial things is not worth telling. Other times the truth is worth hurting feelings. And still other times the truth is better packaged in a way that makes it more palatable for the hearer. The wise dispenser of truth is able to understand the nuances of the context and make good choices concerning sharing the truth with a particular hearer.

Application of the truth is not always as simple as telling the truth all the time. While this is a general maxim society teaches children, there are a few rare examples when speaking the truth actually makes a situation worse. Occasionally, the truth can harm, and it can be intentionally misused to manipulate and distort. When truth is not dispensed with love and compassion, its effect can be disastrous. Thomas Merton made an important observation about the relationship between love and truth when he wrote,

> If men still admire sincerity today, they admire it, perhaps, not for the sake of the truth that it protects, but simply because it is an attractive quality for a person to have. They like to be sincere not because they love the truth, but because, if they are thought to be sincere, people will love them. And perhaps they carry this sincerity to the point of injustice—being too frank about others and themselves, using the truth to fight the truth, and turning it to an instrument of ridicule in order to make others less loved. The "truth" that makes another man seem cheap hides another truth that we should never forget, and which would make him remain always worthy of honor in our sight. To destroy truth with truth under the pretext of being sincere is a very insincere way of telling a lie.[3]

For Merton, truth was to be moderated by love, because not all truth is helpful in a given situation. Hurting people by making them face truth prematurely is *not* a loving approach to relationships. Love is often more important than truth.

Likewise, there are a few rare instances when telling a lie is a more caring action than telling the truth. Look at the parable of "The Good Lie" from the Islamic tradition.

The Good Lie

The king was angry with the foreign captive who had been thrown down before him.

"Put him to death!" he ordered.

The captive had been expecting it. He had up to now been silent but, now that death was certain, he gave up all hope and cursed the king, using the foulest words in his native tongue. He was like a cat, spitting and screeching at dogs who are at its throat.

The king, not knowing the language, did not understand what the captive was screaming, but he knew that one or two of his viziers were familiar with the tongue.

"What is he saying?" he asked them.

The viziers looked at each other. Then, one, who was good-natured, replied: "My lord, he is quoting from the sacred Koran."

"Indeed?" said the king. "From which verse?"

The vizier went on: "From the verse which speaks of the Paradise which awaits those who control their anger and forgive, for God loves men of goodwill."

"I see," said the king, thoughtfully. He turned to the now silent captive. "You have done well to remind me of that," he said. "I will control my anger. And I will forgive you. You can go free."

"That was disgraceful!" muttered another vizier, an enemy and rival of the one who had replied to the king's question. "People of our rank should speak nothing but the truth, particularly before the king."

The king overheard. "What was that?" he asked.

"My lord!" protested the second vizier, "I am sorry, but you were told a lie by that vizier! The captive was certainly not quoting from the Koran. The truth is that he was pouring foul abuse and the filthiest of insults upon you!"

The king frowned at this. "Then I prefer his lie to your truth!" he said. "I think that your truth came from a heart bent upon mischief. His lie came from a good heart, and good has come of it, as you have seen."[4]

By telling a lie to the king, the first vizier was using love to promote a more compassionate outcome for both the captive and the king. The captive would have his life and the king would not have innocent blood on his hands. The vizier's lie was not told frivolously. The vizier was using discretion to reveal the greater truth of the king's own values to the king, himself, in a parabolic way. The vizier rightly discerned that the king would not ordinarily have executed the prisoner if the king had not been filled with rage. By putting wise words in the captive's mouth, the vizier was simply reminding the king of the king's own values. Likewise, the captive reacted to the news of his execution emotionally and lashed out rashly. Simply translating the captive's oaths would have only made the situation worse. The raw truth, in this circumstance, would only inflame more passion and lead to more rash behavior. By telling the lie, the vizier simply smoothed over a tense situation and facilitated the probable happy outcome that would have resulted if emotions had not been so intense. While truth without love can be damaging, a lie told in love can sometimes promote good.

The vizier was risking a lot by intervening with a lie. The vizier *did* get caught, and if the king had not been able to discern that he had indeed kept the king from making a hasty decision that the king would have regretted later, the vizier would likely have been executed as well. The vizier was acting selflessly and had no self-interest in the outcome. But the discretion he used in intervening the way he did served the overall interests of the king, which was his job as vizier in the first place. Using a lie to promote good is a very delicate endeavor and should be reserved for those who understand the personalities and characters of the people involved. Normally, lies are to be avoided because most lies are not told in love. Most lies lead to misunderstanding and harm. Great thought and self-reflection should go into the process of telling a lie to promote a greater good. In most cases, the truth would be more loving. Lies that do not allow the hearer to move to a more mature and compassionate position are probably not appropriate.

Much more can be said on the *contextual use of truth*. However, for the purposes of teaching about parables, one particular aspect of this subject will be explored. When an audience is unsympathetic to the truth, parables can be used to present the truth in a way that maintains the truth's integrity without being offensive. Parables are not always able to accomplish this high intention, but they often have a better outcome than sharing the raw truth alone.

The man in "The Parable of Hypocrisy" was harmed when he was confronted directly with the truth. No loving lie would lead to long-term health for him. But, if he had been presented with the truth in a way that protected his tender ego, he might not have reacted so angrily and the truth could have been used to help him. Since he rejected the raw truth so strongly, he was worse off for having heard it. A plan of sharing the truth with him gradually might have been a more compassionate method of helping him. The man was a hypocrite. Hypocrites often need the truth presented to them in alternative ways in order for them to receive it.

The Use of Parables in Dealing with Hypocrites

There are two primary types of religious hypocrites. There are hypocrites who pretend to be spiritual for a hidden motive, usually self-serving or wicked. A pedophile may become a minister so he can have easy access to children and the cloak of religious authority to throw suspicion off his criminal behavior. A wicked person might become a missionary to toy with people's minds. Another might become a bishop to savor the power that comes with controlling others or selectively destroying those who would truly seek to do good. Jesus warned his followers about these types of hypocrites with these words, "Beware of false prophets, who come to you in sheep's clothing but inwardly are ravenous wolves" (Matt 7:15). While these hypocrites appear to be holy on the outside, their only interest is in consuming the innocent who come to them for instruction and protection. This kind of hypocrite is discerned by their actions. They say one thing and do the opposite for themselves. "Do not steal," they teach the masses, but when no one is watching they take money from the orphan's fund. Wicked hypocrites are very dangerous, not just to the people who are betrayed by trusting them, but because they will often retaliate against anyone who might expose their true natures.

Jesus was crucified by just these kind of hypocrites. Jesus did use parables in dealing with them, but the parables appeared to be as much for the purpose of teaching about hypocrisy to the crowds who overheard Jesus's conversations as it was for the purpose of transforming the wicked. The truly wicked are very difficult to transform. But, even though they are difficult to transform does not mean that they shouldn't be given a final chance for repentance and change. However, the wise teacher counts both the cost of exposing the wicked hypocrite and the cost of offering the transformative moment. Often the cost is safety and life itself. Those not willing to pay such a high price should avoid wicked hypocrites at all costs. They are truly dangerous.

The following is an example of a judicial parable gone awry. Jesus addressed this parable to the chief priests when they confronted him on the day after Palm Sunday as he was teaching in the Jerusalem temple.

The Parable of the Wicked Tenants

"Listen to another parable. There was a landowner who planted a vineyard, put a fence around it, dug a wine press in it, and built a watchtower. Then he leased it to tenants and went to another country. When the harvest time had come, he sent his slaves to the tenants to collect his produce. But the tenants seized his slaves and beat one, killed another, and stoned another. Again he sent other slaves, more than the first; and they treated them in the same way. Finally he sent his son to them, saying, 'They will respect my son.' But when the tenants saw the son, they said to themselves, 'This is the heir; come, let us kill him and get his inheritance.' So they seized him, threw him out of the vineyard, and killed him. Now when the owner of the vineyard comes, what will he do to those tenants?" They said to him, "He will put those wretches to a miserable death, and lease the vineyard to other tenants who will give him the produce at the harvest time."

Jesus said to them, "Have you never read in the scriptures:

'The stone that the builders rejected
has become the cornerstone;
this was the Lord's doing,
and it is amazing in our eyes'?

Therefore I tell you, the kingdom of God will be taken away from you and given to a people that produces the fruits of the kingdom. The one who falls on this stone will be broken to pieces; and it will crush anyone on whom it falls."

When the chief priests and the Pharisees heard his parables, they realized that he was speaking about them. They wanted to arrest him, but they feared the crowds, because they regarded him as a prophet. (Matt 21:33–46)

Jesus told the parable and asked them to pass sentence on the wicked tenants. When the chief priests condemned the tenants, Jesus then brought the judgment back upon them by quoting Psalm 118:22–23. The transformative moment was presented, recognized for what it was, and then rejected. The chief priests immediately began plotting how they would get rid of Jesus. Three days later, Jesus was arrested at night in the Garden of Gethsemane. False witnesses were brought forward at a kangaroo court. He was crucified as a political prisoner the very same day. Judicial parables do not always work. When they don't, the parable teller can be placed in extreme danger. In Jesus's case, Jesus said and did other things to provoke the chief priests, but the "Parable of the Wicked Tenants" was representative of how he interacted with them, and their backroom scheming was typical of how they responded. Those who use parables against wicked hypocrites can expect a similar response. Conversion of the truly wicked is rare.

If confronting wicked hypocrites is so dangerous, the question can be raised, "Why confront them at all?" The answer is because wicked hypocrites left unchecked do great damage to the innocent. Jesus was willing to sacrifice himself in an effort to expose their hypocrisy so the innocent would be spared great pain. Near the end Jesus taught the people directly, "The scribes and the Pharisees sit on Moses's seat; therefore, do whatever they teach you and follow it; but do not do as they do, for they do not practice what they teach" (Matt 23:2–3). In exposing the hypocrisy of religious leaders, Jesus sought to protect the innocent so they would be more cautious in their dealings with these hypocrites. The whole community is harmed if the righteous allow hypocrisy to thrive. The Islamic master Haidar Gul said, "There is a limit beyond which it is unhealthy for mankind to conceal truth in order not to offend those whose minds are closed."[5] There are times when, for the sake of the whole community, wicked hypocrites *must* be stared down even at the risk of personal safety.

When a wicked hypocrite has been approached individually, either directly or through the use of indirect methods, and no hope for repentance or transformation is possible, the religious leader noting the problem should seek help. The most effective approach in limiting the harm inflicted by wicked hypocrites is confronting them with a group of like-minded people who are aware of the damage being done and seeking their removal from the congregation or religious office they hold. In his book, *Clergy Killers: Guidance for Pastors and Congregations Under Attack,* Lloyd Rediger suggests that it is a community problem when someone in a congregation is undermining the leadership of that congregation.[6] Most of the time, the person who is doing the undermining is so entrenched that individual efforts at securing repentance from this person are futile. Only a combined community effort at confronting the person will succeed. And even then, the success usually doesn't result in repentance but drives the person out of the congregation. Such confrontations are always unpleasant, and many congregations have chosen to tolerate the hypocrite's behavior rather than force out the hypocrite. The medicine is unpleasant, but those congregations that directly confront their problem people are healthier in the long run even though they experience loss of membership and unrest in the short run. The religious leader who tries to tackle the wicked hypocrite alone will almost always lose.

The second type of religious hypocrites are those who pretend to be further along on the spiritual journey than they really are. These hypocrites tend to be more pompous than dangerous. Unlike the sheep in wolf's clothing who teaches what is right and knowingly disobeys those teachings, pompous hypocrites sincerely believe they are following the teachings even when they are not. They tend to be more self-deceived than wicked, even though the pain they cause people who trust them is very real. Jesus also dealt with self-deceived hypocrites. On one occasion a rich young man asked him what he had to do to receive eternal life. Jesus told him to obey the commandments. He replied that he had and asked what more he lacked. Jesus then told him to go and sell his possessions and give them to the poor and come and follow him. The rich young man went away sad because he had many possessions (Matt 19:16–22); he truly wanted to be righteous, but he was not willing to pay the price to be so. He left sad, but unlike the wicked hypocrite, he did not go out and plot to murder Jesus because Jesus had exposed his hypocrisy!

Here is a similar example from the Muslim tradition:

Bayazid and the Selfish Man

One day a man reproached Bayazid, the great mystic of the ninth century, saying that he had fasted and prayed and so on for thirty years and not found the joy which Bayazid described. Bayazid told him that he might continue for three hundred years and still not find it.

"How is that?" asked the would-be illuminate.

"Because your vanity is a barrier to you."

"Tell me the remedy."

"The remedy is one which you cannot take."

"Tell me, nevertheless."

Bayazid said: "You must go to the barber and have your (respectable) beard shaved. Remove all your clothes and put a girdle around yourself. Fill a nosebag with walnuts and suspend it from your neck. Go to the marketplace and call out: 'A walnut will I give to any boy who will strike me on the back of the neck.' Then continue on to the justices' session so that they may see you."

"But I cannot do that; please tell me something else that would do as well."

"This is the first move, and the only one," said Bayazid, "but I had already told you that you would not do it; so you cannot be cured."[7]

This parable of El-Ghazali points out that some hypocrites who appear to be quite sincere in seeking spiritual enlightenment are actually motivated by other self-serving reasons: vanity, greed, or respectability. *All* self-serving motives for engaging in the spiritual life are complete barriers to true enlightenment. Until those barriers are broken, self-deceived hypocrites will never find a meaningful relationship with God no matter how sincerely they engage in religious practice.

Parables are the most effective means of helping the self-deceived come to understanding. Direct teaching is rarely effective because self-deceived hypocrites don't lack appropriate *method*, but rather appropriate *motive*, and they keep those motives hidden even from themselves. Jesus didn't ask all of his disciples to give away their possessions to the poor. He only asked the one would-be disciple who cherished riches more than the spiritual life. Likewise, Bayazid did not ask all of his disciples to act like a buffoon, only the disciple who relished public opinion above enlightenment. By reframing the spiritual quest in a way that exposed the self-deceived hypocrites' true motives, each spiritual master was able to bring them to the transformative moment where they had to choose. The rich young man chose his wealth over eternal life. Bayazid's would-be disciple chose respectability over enlightenment. Readers aren't told if these two self-deceived hypocrites changed their minds later; maybe they did. But neither had the potential to progress on their spiritual journeys until their hidden motives were exposed.

Jesus used parables with pompous hypocrites too. In first-century Palestine, individuals would engage in prayer in a public location as a way of displaying their righteousness to others. Concerning the true meaning of confessional prayer, Jesus told the following parable.

The Parable of the Pharisee and Tax Collector

Two men went up to the temple to pray, one a Pharisee and the other a tax collector. The Pharisee, standing by himself, was praying thus, "God, I thank you that I am not like other people: thieves, rogues, adulterers, or even like this tax collector. I fast twice a week; I give a tenth of all my income." But the tax collector, standing far off, would not even look up to heaven, but was beating his breast and saying, "God, be merciful to me, a sinner!" I tell you, this man went down to his home justified rather than the other; for all who exalt themselves will be humbled, but all who humble themselves will be exalted. (Luke 18:10–14)

Prayer, by definition, is communication with God. When people are more concerned with how the prayer sounds to someone overhearing the prayer than about what God thinks of the prayer, then prayer is being misused. Self-deceived hypocrites are concerned with the words of the prayer and whether those words sound better than the prayers of others. They engage in prayer with little thought about their relationships with God. True disciples, on the other hand, do not compare their sins with those of others and find delight in the comparison. Prayers of confession should be about regret for a wrongful deed or attitude, not about taking satisfaction that one's sins are less severe than another's. Jesus's parable reframes the issue of what it means to pray in a way that should convict self-deceived hypocrites of their improper motives.

While self-deceived hypocrites may not be violent in their opposition to those who would help them find release from their self-deception, they are not likely to take such meddling kindly. Parables do have the potential to transform them, but there are many examples when judicial parables did not work. All hypocrites should be treated with caution, and every effort should be made to protect the innocent from the hypocrites' deceit.

I wish there was a simple ten-question multiple-choice test pastors or religious leaders could give to people to determine if they were a self-deceived hypocrite as opposed to a wicked hypocrite. I wish there was a way to predetermine whether a hypocrite would become violent or vindictive if the religious leader exposes their hypocrisy. Unfortunately, there are no such tests available, and the religious leader must use discernment to determine to what extent he wants to try and influence hypocrites. From my own experience, I can say that dealing with hypocrites is always unpleasant. Choosing not to confront them results in an unacceptable status quo. Confronting them and failing creates an enemy. The rare cases when hypocrites change are wonderful. Always remember that God will not protect you from the hypocrite's wrath any more than God protected Jesus from dying on the cross. But, whatever choice you make, to risk confrontation or not, God will love you and comfort you.

Parables and the Audience Hostile to the Speaker's Message

When a teacher or preacher is seeking to convert an audience firmly grounded in a different religious tradition, the use of parables is an ideal way to begin a dialogue about religious concepts. If the teacher is too direct in imparting sectarian doctrine, the audience perceives the intention to convert them and takes offense. The teacher's message is rejected even before the audience has given the new doctrine a fair hearing. Many missionaries from a variety of religious traditions have made this mistake and have been martyred for their efforts. While their intentions may have been noble, they failed in their stated goal of converting their audiences.

Understanding the context within which a teacher is working is a necessary part of communication. Often, a gradual, step-by-step approach to conversion is more effective when trying to reach an audience already well established in a different religious tradition. After building trust and creating friendships with the people, the teacher's next goal is to introduce the basic concepts important to the teacher's religious tradition. Parables are an ideal vehicle for communicating concepts. Teaching that removes specific doctrine from a religious tradition and repackages the concepts within that doctrine in the form of parables is able to teach these ideas without the baggage of the religious tradition. Dialogue about the concept itself can follow. And, only after the audience has accepted the concepts as true can issues about sectarian doctrine be approached.[8]

Mysticism: The art of tasting and feeling in your heart the inner meaning of such stories to the point that they transform you.

Anthony de Mello[1]

8.

HOW TO READ PARABLES FOR TRANSFORMATION

Honesty in Parable Interpretation

Reading the Mystical Text

Six friends decided they were going to start taking their faith more seriously. Each agreed to read the same mystical text, and after a month, they would get back together and share how that text strengthened their faith.

The first friend put the book under her pillow so she could absorb the good vibes emanating from the book. One night she had an erotic dream that she attributed to the book's presence and vowed to find other mystical texts she could experience in the same way. The second friend purchased the book on tape and listened to it in his car as he commuted to work. He had trouble concentrating on what was being said since traffic was often chaotic. He found the book a trifle dry, but believed he got the gist of the argument. The third friend had just finished a speed-reading class and read the entire book in fifteen minutes. He checked it off his reading list and went on to the next. The fourth friend got through the first four pages and found the book too difficult to understand. She decided to read a novel instead, believing that could also improve her faith. The fifth friend formed a study group of other like-minded believers. The discussion was stimulating and helped her see nuances of meaning she had not been able to see reading it by herself. Her study partners challenged her and held her accountable for the changes she promised to make in her life. The sixth friend devoted an hour each day to studying the book. He took a small section at a time and read, reflected, reread, and contemplated how he could bring his life into conformity with the concepts in the book. He hadn't finished the entire book at the end of the month, but he vowed he would spend the rest of his life reading it.

At the end of the month all six friends reported that they had gained a lot by reading this mystical text. Each reported having a stronger faith! Alas, if only it were true!

In the preface to his book of parables, *Half-Told Tales,* Henry Van Dyke acknowledged that reading parables requires work on the part of the reader.

> It grieves me to the heart to have to make a singular, and perhaps presumptuous, request of the readers of this book, if perchance it finds any. Will you kindly do a bit of thinking while you read? Otherwise these Half-Told Tales will mean nothing to you. The worth of a book depends on the reader as much as on the writer.[2]

People read for many different reasons. They read for relaxation and entertainment. They read to gain information. They read to be moved and inspired. Each type of reading requires a different attitude and a different kind of "work" to get something out of the reading. Readers who bring the wrong attitude to a particular piece of literature usually don't understand the author's intentions. A student who does not concentrate on the textbook will not retain the information. A tense, agitated person may not find a novel relaxing if he remains fixated on the cause of his anger. A monk who skims a religious text is not likely to be moved. Authors generally give clues to help readers know what kind of effort will be required to master a particular literary work. Authors of textbooks underline main points requiring memorization. Nonfiction writers explain the purpose of their work in a preface. Novelists tell entertaining stories. Fabulists leave the reader with a concluding proverb or moral. At the very least, the genre of literature itself gives readers a hint as to the type of work required to read it. Henry Van Dyke moved beyond the subtle hint and bluntly asked his readers to think about the half-told tales they were about to read. He intended his stories to be more thought provoking than entertaining.

Van Dyke was also correct when he asserted that the worth of a literary work depends upon the reader as much as the author. Of course, this comment is made from an author's perspective. An author wants readers to get his message. The primary success of the work from the author's point of view depends upon whether readers understand the author's intended meaning. However, authors lose control of the message once the work is published and dispersed. Readers seize control of the language event when they pick up a literary work out of the author's earshot. They read the work with their own needs in mind. After all, different kinds of literature can be read in ways not intended by an author. Educational texts can be read for entertainment. Information can be gleaned from inspirational literature. Novels can be read to evoke an emotional response. Despite the best attempts of authors to steer readers toward a proper understanding of their works, the reader is the one who determines what will be taken away from the language event of reading a particular piece of literature.

In "Reading the Mystical Text," six readers approached a particular book using six different methods. The author of this unnamed religious text would probably be appalled at the way some of the readers used the book. The author has the right to be appalled. However, readers also have a right to explore a text in nontraditional ways. If they take away insight, humor, or, in the case of the first friend, erotic dreams, then the literary work had an unintended effect. As long as that effect doesn't *hurt* anyone else, what does it matter?

While readers do have a right to find unintended uses for literary works, they also have a responsibility to be honest with themselves and others about what they got from a particular piece of literature. For instance, the fourth friend should have been honest with the group and admitted she didn't understand the mystical text and gave up reading it after four pages. If her faith was stronger at the end of the month it wasn't because of this specific book. Readers need to be honest with themselves, not only about what they got out of a particular text, but also about the methodology they used when reading it. If they purposefully read it against the intention of the author, they have at least been honest about their actions. But, if they either intentionally or unintentionally sabotage the language event by not putting the right kind of effort into reading it, or worse, misrepresent what they got out of it, then those readers are to be pitied. They have shown no integrity in the reading process.

Reading parables generally requires more work than other types of literature. It not only demands cognitive thought, but also an intentional openness to allowing the parable to sink into the subconscious. According to Halqavi, one of the Sufi masters and author of *The Food of Paradise,* most parables do not affect the "inner consciousness" of hearers in a beneficial way unless they are open to being touched. He believes most people find in parables only what they expect to find: entertainment, puzzlement, allegory. He states that how, where, and when a parable is studied in the faith development of hearers has a tremendous influence on whether they will find enlightenment from reading it.[3] Developing this attitude of openness is part of the "work" required to read parables.

Sometimes, the subconscious is penetrated by a parable because the hearer was caught off guard. This does indeed happen. But a person who goes into the language event of reading parables precisely in order to be touched and transformed usually has to work at developing an attitude of openness for those language events to bear fruit on a regular basis. Like other types of literature, parables don't have to be read for transformation; they can be read for entertainment. Halqavi asserts, in fact, that most people don't "get" the intended point. Therefore, those who want more than the occasional "caught off guard" experience with parables need to learn how to work at reading parables. Techniques are available to assist the serious student in cultivating the process for personal transformation. But before we explore them, let's briefly examine the variety of ways interpreters can approach parables.

Categories of Interpretation

Hermeneutics is the discipline of how texts are properly interpreted. The English word *hermeneutic* is a transliteration of the Greek word *hermeneuein,* nominally meaning "to interpret." The Greek word, in turn, is derived from the name of the Greek god, Hermes, who as the messenger of the gods was responsible for making the divine message intelligible to humanity. In religious circles, hermeneutics focuses on finding the divine meaning of religious texts. More generally, hermeneutics is simply the process of deciphering what words mean. In addition to religious texts, literary texts can be examined using a variety of hermeneutical methods. Not all are equally applicable to the interpretation of parables. While volumes of books have been devoted to hermeneutics from the time of Aristotle until the present, readers should know that this chapter only brushes upon hermeneutical principles applicable to parables. We will start with interpretive intention, which is at the heart of where hermeneutics begins. Why is the parable being interpreted at all?

Impersonal Interpretation versus Personal Interpretation

The interpretation of parables can be divided into two broad categories: impersonal and personal. *Impersonal interpretations* are those that seek to provide meaning and insight to others. The interpreter of a parable becomes the unbiased purveyor of truth to ignorant hearers. Attempting to be unbiased, the interpreter makes note of the context of the parable and the context of the hearers and proposes an interpretation that she believes will be informative to those who cannot understand the parable without help. The interpreter is detached from the parable itself and also from its application. Helping others find meaning from the parable is more important than the interpreter finding meaning for herself.

On the other hand, *personal interpretations* of parables are those in which hearers seek to find personal edification and insight from the parable for themselves. Hearers are not concerned *how* a parable is understood by others, but remain focused on *what* the parable means to them. Hearers might consult the works of those engaged in the practice of impersonal interpretation in their quest to understand the meaning of a particular parable, but any interpretations not relevant for their own contexts are quickly discarded as they seek the meaning that speaks directly to them.

Of course, these two positions are extreme and many interpreters can fall in between the extremes. The process can be graphed on a one-dimensional number line with the unmitigated impersonal interpretation forming one pole and unmitigated personal interpretation forming the other. Hearers of parables can chart the degree of their intentions graphically (see Figure 1). Some might be interested in teaching others and open to finding personal meaning too. They would be represented by point "A." Others might be more interested in the personal meaning, but would be open to sharing that meaning. Their intentions would be represented by point "B." Those who were equally interested in teaching others and finding meaning for themselves would be located at the origin of the graph denoted by "Both."

FIGURE 1. Interpretive Intention Graphed Linearly

| Impersonal | A | Both | B | Personal |

In all impersonal interpretive approaches, the interpreter stands between the parable and the hearers. The interpreter brokers the meaning the parable is able to have, and hearers are as much influenced by the interpreter as the parable itself. In the best case scenario, the interpreter is a bridge allowing hearers full access to the parable and its meanings. Otherwise, the interpreter is a gate, controlling which meanings are allowed to go between the parable and hearers, encouraging some meanings and discouraging others.

Parable interpreters do have their place. Without them, some hearers would never get the point. As long as interpreters have the best interests of the hearers in mind, the process is usually a beneficial one for all. However, interpreters can easily fall into the trap of either paternalistically believing they know what is best for a given set of hearers or mistakenly believing that an interpretation that has meaning for them will be equally valid for others. Interpreters who think they stand on the far left side of the graph and honestly believe they are completely unbiased can do great damage when those who listen to their interpretations are unaware of the interpreters' self-interest. Realistically, interpreters never can be completely free of self-interest in the interpretation process and they deceive themselves if they think they can be completely neutral. Interpreters are far better off admitting what's in it for themselves up front. If they enjoy helping other people find enlightenment, that is well and good, but if they have a vested interest in excluding a particular interpretation and work toward discouraging that interpretation in hearers, then woe be to them. Jesus called such interpreters blind guides. "If one blind person guides another, both will fall into a pit" (Matt 15:14). Interpreters who misuse their authority and push false interpretations of parables onto hearers do great damage. This warning goes beyond interpreters of religious parables. I've seen high school English teachers and professors of literature misuse their interpretive authority for self-interest as well. To have integrity, interpreters need to be in touch with their own motivations and issues and freely disclose those facts to hearers. Interpreters who spend time with Figure 1 ascertaining the degree to which they allow the parable to speak to them are more likely to be bridges for others. Graphing intention helps in the process of sorting out motives.

Literal Interpretation versus Figurative Interpretation

Hermeneutically, it is within the realm of possibility that parables can be interpreted literally. With the rise of fundamentalism in world religions where leaders encourage followers to read religious texts literally, this possibility needs to be addressed. Parables are *not* "literal" literature. To read most parables literally is to entirely miss the author's intended point, and can even do great damage to hearers. Let's look at an example.

Soaring Like Eagles

Two students climbed a lofty mountain to visit the sage who lived in a cave near the top of the mountain. Having finally arrived, the first student asked, "O wise sage, how do we discern God's will for our lives?"

After contemplating a moment, the sage replied, "To speak with God you must ascend to heaven soaring like the mighty eagle."

Both students bowed to the sage and exited the cave. The first student immediately sat down on a rock, closed his eyes in contemplation, and visualized himself as an eagle flying higher and higher into the heavens. The second student climbed up the mountain a little farther, flapped his arms and ran around screaming as he had once heard an eagle scream. After a time, the second student returned to see how his friend had made out.

The first student exclaimed, "I have spoken with God!"

"Good," said the second student. "What did God say?"

"God said we should go out and fish for people."

"Ah," said the second student, "I've got two rods at home, but we'll have to buy larger hooks and stronger line."

Metaphorical speech, when interpreted literally, can lead to absurdity as it does in the parable of "Soaring Like Eagles." The second student is sincere in his literal approach to finding God, even if he is misguided. But imagine the damage this misguided student will do when he takes a fishing rod and starts hooking people at the mall with real fish hooks! Fortunately, most people are not so obtuse, but some are, and this warning is raised for their benefit. Taking a religious text *seriously* is very different from taking it *literally*. Sometimes, to take a text seriously, it must be understood *figuratively* as it was intended. *Parables are figurative literature.*

There are different degrees of being figurative. If the reference point for determining the degree of being figurative is the literal interpretation, then this process can also be graphed on a one-dimensional number line (see Figure 2). An analogy is closer to being literal than a metaphor; a metaphor is closer to being literal than an allegory; and an allegory is closer to being literal than a symbol. At the end of the figurative scale is the abstraction, which becomes less recognizable as it becomes even more abstract. On the literal side of the scale, the farther one moves to the left, the closer the words become the thing signified by the words.

FIGURE 2. The Figurativeness of a Text Graphed Linearly

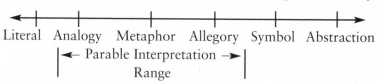

The most common range on the graph for the interpretation of parables runs from analogy through allegory with metaphor at the center. Parables can be an analogy. Take Jesus's "Parable of the Leaven" as an example: "The kingdom of heaven is *like* yeast that a woman took and mixed in with three measures of flour until all of it was leavened" (Matt 13:33, emphasis added). The parable is structured as a simple analogy with the word *like* signaling the process of analogy. The kingdom of heaven is to be compared with the process of leavening bread, but they are *not* equivalent. The process of leavening bread provides one single insight into what the kingdom of heaven is *like*. Analogy is a weaker comparison than metaphor. And a metaphor using the words *like* or *as* is known as a simile. Compare "love is *like* a rose" with "love *is* a rose." In the former a single insight about love is made, while in the latter love is made equivalent with the rose. In metaphor the subjects are stated as being equivalent. The strength of comparison being made in a particular parable needs to be considered in interpreting that parable. Parables using analogy for comparison are weaker than parables using metaphor. The "Parable of the Leaven" also uses the tale style even though it is only one sentence in length.

At the other end of the range, allegory requires access to the hidden code that unlocks its meaning. The parable's hearer must recognize the parable is in allegory style in order to find the intended meaning. The style of the parable signals how the parable should be approached within the figurative realm. Allegories can be constructed that are not parables, so care should be exercised in discerning type and function of a literary allegory when seeking to interpret it. Likewise, not all analogies are parables, and for that matter, not all metaphors are parables.

The value of thinking about the level of figurativeness of a particular literary text is in the proper methodology used to examine the text further. Particularly, to those prone to looking at all religious literature literally, the process of consciously standing back and assessing the figurativeness of the text gives insight into the interpretative approach that should be used.

Allegorical Interpretation versus Metaphorical Interpretation

In order to access the meaning of a parable intended by its author, parables that are analogies should be interpreted as analogies; parables that are metaphors should be interpreted as metaphors; and parables that are allegories should be interpreted as allegories. However, just as literature can be read in ways not intended by an author, parables can be interpreted in ways not intended as well. One such methodology is the *allegorical approach*. This approach forces an allegorical meaning upon a parable that is more properly a metaphor. A parable can be interpreted allegorically when elements in the parable are assumed to represent something else symbolically. Dan Otto Via rightly points out that a distinction should be made between interpreting a parable that is a true allegory and giving an allegorical interpretation of a parable that is not in itself allegorical. A true allegory should be understood symbolically as it was intended. Allegorically interpreting a parable that was not intended to be an allegory superimposes a meaning on the parable that might not have been intended by its original teller.[4] In the Christian tradition, the allegorical approach was the predominant method used to interpret Jesus's parables until the early twentieth century. Though this approach has fallen out of favor with most Christian scholars, the allegorical approach has its place and can be used to convey truth to hearers. However, the allegorical approach can be used to obscure truth as well and caution should be exercised in approaching metaphorical parables allegorically.

Heinz Politzer outlined three different allegorical approaches to interpreting Franz Kafka's parables.[5] All three approaches are impersonal interpretations and can be generalized and adapted for use on any parable. First, an interpreter can explain the meaning of a parable historically. The context of the parable is assumed to be the political or historical situation in which the author of the parable lived. The parable is presumed to be a covert political commentary on the society at large. The task of the interpreter is to make the historical context of the parable clear so that hearers can get an accurate insight into how the original audience must have heard the parable. The interpreter makes parallels between the original context and the current contexts in which the secondary hearers live so they might find meaning for themselves.

Second, an interpreter can explain the meaning of a parable psychologically. The context of hearers is assumed to be a personal struggle for meaning or the solving of interpersonal or intrapersonal problems. The interpreter points out ways in which the parable parallels the lives of hearers and suggests they can act in the same ways as the parable's main characters. The interpreter must know a great deal about the personal lives of the hearers she is seeking to influence for this method to be effective.

Third, an interpreter can explain the meaning of a parable biographically. The assumption is that hearers are interested in understanding the context of the author so they might gain insight into the author's life. Interpreters usually must have access to personal information about a parable's author in order to attempt a biographical interpretation.

Primary Meanings versus Secondary Meanings

While a few parables are analogies and allegories, most parables are metaphorical stories. Usually, the entire story itself is the metaphor. When the situation described in the parable can be laid out beside another situation and the two situations illuminate one another, then the parable has a primary meaning. A parable can have more than one primary meaning if it can be laid beside other situations and insight can be drawn. "The Parable of the Mediocre Life" in chapter 4 would necessarily bring different responses from individuals depending upon whether they could relate more easily to Mr. Mediocre or to Mr. Brilliant. Someone who could relate to Mr. Mediocre might experience pain, sadness, and regret that he has consistently made safe choices throughout his life rather than having taken risks to follow his dreams. He correctly interpreted the parable according to its primary meaning that mediocrity is damaging. However, a woman who could relate more easily to Mr. Brilliant might experience relief and comfort in her context because she has personally experienced persecution from mediocre colleagues. She takes comfort that her job termination was not because *she* was inadequate, but because her workplace was inadequate. She also correctly interpreted the parable according to its primary meaning that standouts in society are often mistreated.

Beyond that, parables can have secondary meanings. Secondary meanings arise when parts of a parable can be laid beside other situations and insights can be drawn even when the metaphor of the entire parable does not exactly fit with the situation to which it is being compared. For example, take "The Lost Penny" from chapter 4. The primary meaning of the parable involves the priority of wealth in happiness. However, a mother who reads the parable might become intrigued with the relationship that has been built between Tom and his uncle during the walks they have taken together Tom's whole life. She might gain insight into how to improve her relationship with one of her children. She might even intentionally plan to take her son on long walks to allow him to express himself and strengthen their mother-son relationship. The parable does have a subtheme involving relationship. As the uncle became wealthier, the walks with Tom became more infrequent and their relationship grew more distant. The mother, reading the parable, might latch onto the subtheme and find it life changing even if the primary theme of wealth is not relevant for her situation. The parable had a secondary meaning that for her may be profound. The categorization of primary and secondary meanings for the sake of interpreting parables does not mean that the insight gained from a primary meaning is more powerful than that gained from a secondary meaning. Rather, the designations primary and secondary are from the author's perspective of what was originally intended. Secondary, or unintended, meanings should not be thought of as lesser meanings. Many secondary meanings can be gleaned from a parable using the allegorical approach to interpretation.

Reading Parables for Personal Enlightenment

Parables can be studied using the hermeneutical principles outlined above. A parable can be categorized and analyzed based on its literary type and style. Background research can be done on the author of the parable and the historical background in which the parable is set. Books interpreting parables can be consulted. The primary meaning of the parable can be stated based upon the student's study of the parable. Secondary meanings can be explored using the allegorical method. The result of such study provides intellectual understanding and even enlightenment if the student vows to incorporate the meaning of the parable into his life. Studying parables can provide sought-after transformation.

A less intellectual approach to reading parables can also provide transformation when hearers intentionally allow their subconscious to discern the meaning of a parable for themselves. Any of a number of meditative approaches to reading religious literature are effective when applied to parables. Those who regularly practice a meditative discipline can incorporate the reading of parables into their daily meditations looking for transformative experiences. For those less experienced in meditation, let me suggest one method based upon the Christian tradition's *lectio divina*. *Lectio divina* is Latin for *divine reading*. Originally, it was a contemplative way of reading scripture searching for an encounter with the divine. Through the centuries the process of *lectio divina* has been described in a number of ways and no process of standardization has been attempted, nor is that even seen as valuable. Because of personality issues, meditative practice necessarily must be individualized. The method I describe is one adaptation for use with nonscriptural parables. The process has six steps.

1. Relaxation
2. Reading
3. Meditation
4. Interaction
5. Contemplation
6. Reflection

Readers should feel free to experiment and personalize this method for their own use.

Reading for personal enlightenment is time consuming. Readers should not hurry the process. If readers are not willing to devote an adequate amount of time to the reading process, they short-circuit the benefits they might have gained by engaging their subconscious in the process. Every reader has different needs and individual time constraints, so there are no time boundaries set by the process itself. However, the reader should not feel rushed or the process is hampered.

First, before engaging in the process of reading parables for personal enlightenment, you should take adequate time to *relax*. Breathing and stretching exercises, mantra chanting, or a process of meditative calming are all techniques that can be used to help yourself disengage from the distractions around you and get more in touch with your inner self. Soft instrumental music playing in the background helps some people relax and drowns out background noise that might be disturbing. Others find the music itself distracting. The place or time of day also can be important in making the experience more meaningful. Some places might promote a feeling of security more than others. Likewise, certain people find meditative exercises more fulfilling if done in the morning as a way of setting the tone for the entire day. Others prefer the end of the day as a wrap-up. Find the right combination that works for you. Again, relaxation takes time and readers need to be comfortable and feel safe before they begin.

Second, *read the parable slowly*, allowing the words to become thoughts and images in your mind. Reread the parable as many times as it takes to become completely familiar with the story. Put the text down and retell the parable as if you were relating it to someone else. Ultimately, you want the parable to become part of you.

Third, when you are completely familiar with the parable, close your eyes and *meditate* upon the story. Let your mind wander over the elements of the story. If particular parts of the story are more interesting than others, let your subconscious explore those possibilities. If distractions that are not part of the parable come into your mind, acknowledge them and release them so you can return back to the parable. You might visualize or imagine the parable being played in your mind like a drama. Savor the experience in your meditation.

Fourth, after you are completely immersed in the parable, try to *interact* with the parable. Put yourself into the story as an observer. Try talking to the main characters; ask them questions and wait for their responses. If your subconscious does not supply an answer right away or at all, don't despair! Move on to another character, or thank them for their silence and their presence with you. You might try asking the characters for advice. Ask them to help you understand their actions. Listen patiently without arguing with them. You might not like some of the answers you get. Don't be too quick to dismiss the implications of what the characters tell you. The characters are simply a manifestation of your own subconscious, and their responses are the part of you that you hide from yourself. Try not to think about the implications of their answers now. There will be time afterward to cognitively sort out the insights that came through meditation. This is the time to collect insights for later.

Fifth, after you have exhausted your questions, enter into a time of *contemplation*. Seek to clear your mind of all thoughts and experience a time of rest and peace. As thoughts intrude upon your rest, acknowledge and dismiss them. Meditation and interaction with the parable can be emotionally draining, and the contemplation time allows you to rest from the experience and find peace.

Finally, spend a few moments in *reflection* upon what you learned in your encounter with the parable. Sort through the insights gained and see if you can summarize the meaning of the parable for yourself. If you keep a diary or journal, you might want to jot down a few insights for later. List the changes you can make in your life based upon your encounter with the parable. Share your insights with a trusted friend or spiritual advisor. Your friend can provide encouragement and a memory of the event so the insights you gained won't be lost. Friendship provides accountability for change and loving support.

Not Getting It: When the Meaning Is Elusive

Parables are a lot like jokes. Hearers either get the punch line or they don't. Those who don't immediately get the punch line usually don't find the joke funny even after it has been explained. The part of the brain that enjoys humor doesn't appear to be connected to the cerebral part that processes information. So, understanding why a particular joke is supposed to be funny does not always incite laughter. Likewise, intellectually understanding the moral of a parable does not always lead to a personally transformative experience. The intellectual part of the brain is separate from the subconscious that responds to personal insight. When the subconscious part of the brain that controls insight is shut down, no amount of explanation or commentary will make a particular parable transformative.

Sometimes readers will encounter a parable they instinctually know has a hidden meaning for them, but no matter how hard they try, they cannot seem to unlock that meaning for themselves. Don't give up. Read the parable every day for a month if need be. Meditate on it. Study it. Dissect it. Read commentaries on it. Ask a friend to read it with you and get her input on its meaning. Use every method available to discern that parable's meaning. That parable may have the power to transform your life. Parables do have the power to transform! And, those who persevere will eventually find that meaning. Their subconscious will drop its guard one day and the meaning will be made clear. When that happens, it is truly a mystical experience.

If readers pour their hearts into understanding a parable, and after a long period of meditation, study, and thought, a meaning *still* does not materialize, then let it go. Put the parable aside for awhile and come back to it with more life experience. Some parables have different messages for people at various stages in their lives. Some parables may never reveal their message to certain hearers. The goal of reading parables should not be to intellectually understand every one that is read, but to be moved and transformed by a few of them. And to be transformed by a few, hearers have to read many of them. When those few transformative moments happen, words cannot describe the wonder and majesty of those mystical insights.

The back matter includes an annotated bibliography of collections of parables that readers can use to practice reading parables for personal transformation.

Parables have a way of sneaking up on us, appealing to our secret senses, and delighting us in their simplicity of truth. One does not have to be a scholar or an academic to appreciate a parable. In fact, a literal mind is often an impediment to understanding a parable. Rather, what is required is a childlike imagination and the ability to think metaphorically.   Todd Outcalt[1]

9.

HOW TO WRITE PARABLES FOR TRANSFORMATION

The Right Motivation for Changing Others

Two women had been trying to get their husbands to quit smoking for years. The first wasn't so much concerned about her husband's health as she was about the extra annoyance his cigarette smoke caused her. The second was genuinely worried about the well-being of her husband, and she would love him to the end whether he quit smoking or not. Together they decided to craft a parable in the hopes it would inspire their husbands to quit smoking. This is the fruit of their effort.

The Parable of the Leftover Life

There were twin brothers who were virtually inseparable from birth. They liked all the same things and did everything together. The only difference between them was one started smoking at age twelve, while the other never did. They lived full lives together, the best of friends.

The brother who smoked died at age seventy. His twin was devastated. Every day he thought about his brother and missed him. But, life goes on, and he continued to do all the things they had enjoyed together.

After the second brother died at age seventy-five, his daughter found a list. The list contained a catalog of activities followed by a long string of slash marks seeming to indicate the number of times he had done those things. Out of curiosity, she added up the marks, and then she decided to type up the list and give it to the first brother's family. This is just part of the list: 62 fishing trips; 5 Christmases with family; 258 movies at the theater on Friday night watching the teenagers fall in love with their dates; 1,825 walks at the mall; 10 vacations, one to the Grand Canyon; 520 intimate encounters with my wife; 563 sunsets enjoyed on the porch with my dog; being there when my great-grandson was born; two family weddings; and my brother's funeral. At the bottom of the list was a note to his departed brother, "Dearest brother, I miss you so much. Every time I do anything that we used to do, I mark it down on this list. I figure that since we had the same genetics and lived identical lifestyles, the only difference in our longevity is that you were a smoker and I wasn't. This list consists of all the things I did with my leftover life. If I had been a smoker, these are the things I would have had to give up."

The first woman planned to use the parable as bait in a judicial parable trap. She was waiting for the right opportunity, but before one presented itself she went into one of her self-righteous speeches after his secondhand smoke got into her eyes. She presented the parable, but he laughed. He understood she was annoyed by the smoke—and didn't care.

The second woman carefully set her trap over a romantic dinner in a nice restaurant. After they had agreed they would do this more often, she gave him the parable and told him she had written it. He was moved—but he didn't quit smoking right away. Over the next year he struggled to cut back, and finally, with help from a physician and a support group, he was able to beat his addiction. His wife loved him through the whole process and continually reaffirmed how much she wanted "more" life with him as much as "quality" life. The parable made up only one piece of his decision to quit, but it was an important piece.

In the above example, the first woman was only interested in changing her husband for selfish reasons. She didn't like the extra cleaning necessitated by living with a smoker, and she didn't like the secondhand smoke. Since she wasn't particularly concerned about her husband's health, her selfish motives were clear. Her husband saw the parable as just another attempt to nag him.

The second woman loved her husband and out of that love wanted him to stop smoking. She was prepared to love him even if he didn't quit. Her love was unconditional. Because we know the motives of the two women, ethical judgments can be made concerning their efforts. We can say the first woman was being manipulative because she only had self-serving reasons for trying to change her husband. However, because the second woman had her husband's best interests in mind, when she attempted to change him, she was ethically within the bounds of being appropriate.

People attempt to change and influence people every day. Every time a parent punishes a child, a boss gives feedback to an employee, a student attends a classroom lecture, a bank robber threatens a teller, an angry shopper complains to a store manager, a teen pressures his girlfriend for sex, or a respondent replies to a survey, attempts are being made to change someone. Some of these changes are motivated by the purest intentions. Other attempts are self-serving, even harmful. Most of the time, people try to change or influence others without giving a thought to whether their reasons are selfish or selfless.

There are times when selfish motives serve the common good. The drowning man selfishly screams to a passerby to save him. A suicidal teenager inconveniences a teacher when she asks him to take her to the hospital. A girl asks her brother to intervene with the bully who is teasing her. Not all self-serving requests are inappropriate. Likewise, not every selfless request is appropriate. However, those who reflect on their motives for seeking to influence others and sincerely try to influence them for noble reasons do good. Parables, like all other forms of persuasion, should only be used for noble reasons.

Thinking Metaphorically

Those who want to use parables must begin to think metaphorically when they communicate with others. The simple process of thinking metaphorically involves using analogies or metaphors to help someone else understand a concept. Being able to think metaphorically and to offer solutions to problems in this way is an essential quality for those who want to use parables. Students can't solve calculus problems until they fully grasp algebra. Parables are simply an advanced form of metaphorical thinking. For instance, middle-aged men who find themselves in the hospital for the first time frequently have a hard time understanding why they got sick and are frustrated laying in bed. As a pastor I look for an analogy they can understand to make their hospital stay more tolerable. Take this conversation fragment as an example of solving a problem with a simple metaphor:

"You take your truck in for a tune-up and leave it at the garage overnight don't you?" I say.

The man in the hospital bed answers, "Sure, a clean engine runs better and lasts longer."

"Think of your hospital stay as a tune-up for your body. The mechanic—I mean doctor—will get your problem under control and you'll be back to work in no time. But, while you're here, be cooperative and open your hood willingly. The human body needs an occasional tune-up, too."

The blue-collar macho-man understands the metaphor and lays back in the hospital bed and relaxes. I've used this metaphor dozens of time with "motorheads" in the hospital and it works. They *do* relax and tend to be more cooperative after I've reframed what their hospital stay means in terms of an engine tune-up. Of course, not every man is a "motorhead." While the metaphor is still intellectually grasped by people who don't like to work on their own cars, the metaphor works more powerfully with those who do. Metaphors that strike closest to home are the most effective.

Using simple metaphors to solve problems is the most basic form of parabolic transformation. People using a metaphor need to have a fairly good knowledge of the audience to use this method for promoting understanding. They need to find some subject to which their audience can relate easily that will shed insight into the problem at hand. People developing a metaphor need to think about the problem from the audience's point of view. They need to imagine they were in the same situation and consider which metaphor would help the audience reframe this problem so the audience can come to understanding. Being able to solve problems with simple metaphors or analogies is the first step toward solving problems with parables. Parable stories are simply complex metaphors that are used to solve more stubborn problems.

A Process of Developing Parables

Writing parables is a creative act, and as with all creative endeavors there is a variety of ways the task can be done. There is not a right or wrong way to create art. In this chapter I will outline the process I use in writing parables. This is not the *only* way, but it is the method that works for me and I commend it to others.

First, parables are indirect forms of persuasion. They should only be used when direct communication has failed or there is a compelling reason not to be direct. Many people are reluctant to speak directly to someone they love about sensitive issues. Most of the time a frank conversation held in a loving atmosphere will accomplish the sought-after goal. In the conversation, be sure to show respect for the person. Express your desire to reach a mutually satisfactory solution to the presenting problem. Decide to unconditionally love the person regardless of the outcome. Make the person feel safe and loved before addressing the sensitive issue. How the sensitive issue is approached is almost as important as discussing the issue itself.

However, if the direct approach has already failed and the person is exhibiting behavior consistent with being willfully disobedient, stubborn, self-deceived, or callously ignorant, or if there is a disparity of power between you, then the parabolic approach is warranted. The parabolic approach is always appropriate when used with groups to present a teaching metaphor or an example metaphor.

For me, the conception of a parable begins with a presenting problem. As a religious leader, I am frequently challenged to explain esoteric religious concepts. Take as an example the Christian doctrine of the incarnation that teaches God's Word became flesh and dwelt among us. There are certainly good theological books available that rationally explain this doctrine, but the intellectual answers are often unsatisfying to congregants. Sermons or lessons only using textbook answers to explain difficult theological questions are often dry, boring, and ineffective because congregants cannot seem to internalize the answer and make it part of their faith. Being able to recite a memorized answer is far different from sharing the answer out of genuine belief because the answer has been internalized in faith. A dispassionate teacher might be satisfied with the former, but a preacher strives for the latter state. So the stated problem for this example is how to inspire congregants to experience the doctrine of the incarnation instead of being lectured about it.

Now that the presenting problem has been identified, the context of the congregants needs to be evaluated to find the right story that will resonate with these particular congregants. What setting for the parable will work so they will immediately identify with the parable? Picking a setting not too far away from where the people live is important. Rural settings for urban congregants who have only seen pictures of farms just don't connect. The resulting story might be cute, but it won't be parabolic if the metaphorical images raised do not stir their subconscious minds to action. A thorough knowledge of the audience is essential for matching the context of the parable with the context of the audience. For this example, the audience is a mostly Caucasian, suburban, Christian congregation. Since incarnation deals with words, and words form lectures or sermons, one context in which the parable itself might be set is a preaching event. If the principle metaphor of the parable was a preaching event, these congregants would be able to relate to the parable.

When the context has been evaluated and the predominant metaphor for the parable has been selected, the parable itself is created incorporating all the elements that make a story parabolic. The working definition of parables from chapter 1 states: "Parables become transformative language events when brief, metaphorically shocking stories covertly bring about insight into a difficult subject, covertly provide a model for hearers to imitate, or covertly inspire a change of heart in the hearers because their own life situations, when compared to that of the stories, are found wanting." With the working definition of parables in mind, we run through the checklist of seven characteristics of parables and make sure the created work is truly a parable. In this example, we have already evaluated the context (characteristic 6), and desire the story (characteristic 1) to be transformative (characteristic 4). We have selected the primary metaphor for the story (characteristic 2): laying side by side the doctrine of the incarnation with a preaching event. The covert nature of the parable (characteristic 7) will be addressed in the parable's delivery. All that is left is to create a parable that is brief (characteristic 3) and make sure the resulting story has an unexpected twist or surprise (characteristic 5).

Furthermore, in the creation process, a literary style should be chosen for the parable from the fifteen examples in chapters 4 and 5. Some styles lend themselves better than others for certain situations. Being thoroughly familiar with each of the styles gives the parable writer a form or model in which to create the parable. Because tale-style parables work well for teaching-metaphor parables, it has been selected for this example.

Even though parables are short, I still take time to outline the work before I start. Outlining helps me organize the basic concepts I want included in the parable so they are presented in a way that is truly parabolic. Sometimes my outline is very rough; just a few sentences or phrases to fix the order and determine where the twist will occur. The outline also helps me determine exactly how much information I need to make the parable work. Usually, this stage is where I make decisions about the primary details that must be included for the story to be coherent. At the rough draft stage of the parable, I compare the parable to the outline to make sure the project is still on track. Occasionally, the outline needs to be modified to accommodate a new insight, but usually if there is a discrepancy between the outline and the rough draft, it is the rough draft that gets modified. The outline is only for my benefit, and I always throw it away as the finished parable is printing.

There is much debate among writers about the value of out-lining. Many excellent writers never formally write out an outline for their work even though they do have it mentally mapped out in their minds. Outlines are just a technique writers use to organize their thoughts before writing the first draft. Outlines work particularly well with beginning writers because when the work is structurally laid out in outline form, mistakes are easier to detect and fix before a lot of effort is expended.

Here is an outline for the example parable.

Title: The Word Became Flesh

I. Introductory Question.

A. Student comes to teacher with question.

1. "How can words possibly become something solid like flesh?"

B. The story to follow is the answer.

II. Great teacher speaks to crowd.

A. (The teacher is aged and crippled so that he is no longer able to put into action what he believes. He will be contrasted with the young, able hearer who can do what the aged teacher cannot.)

B. Word is sent into the air at the preaching event.

1. Care for poor.

2. Feed the hungry.

3. Love neighbors.

III. Young female student hears message.

A. (There will be a one-to-one correspondence between the points in the teacher's message and the volunteer activities of the hearer.)

B. Word is received and transformed into action.

    1. Volunteer at women's shelter.

    2. Organize food pantry.

    3. Help neighbor learn to read.

IV. Conclusion.

A. The parabolic twist comes when the teacher's beliefs are put into action through the young woman's volunteer activities and is summarized with the explanatory comment about how words can become flesh.

    1. "The teacher's words became flesh through the young woman's actions."

Here is the resulting parable.

The Word Became Flesh

A student came to the Master Teacher and asked, "Master Teacher, I have read in the scriptures, 'And the Word became flesh and lived among us,' but I do not understand what it means. Words are carried through the air. How can words possibly become something solid like flesh?"

After contemplating a moment, the Master Teacher replied, "The answer to your confusion is found in the following story. A young woman went to hear a great teacher speak at a local church. The aged teacher, whose body was crippled and broken, slowly walked up behind the pulpit. But his voice boomed with power and enthusiasm. He proclaimed his message, 'Care for the poor! Feed the hungry! Love your neighbors!' The great teacher's message got through to that young woman, and she walked away a changed person.

"Immediately, the young woman went to a local women's and children's shelter and volunteered her time to play with the lonely children. She found other like-minded people in her community and revitalized the local food pantry. A man who lived on her street was illiterate. She worked with him until he could read. The message of the great teacher had a profound effect upon the young woman. The teacher's words became flesh through the young woman's actions. Let the one who has ears hear."

Because the parable is intended to be a teaching-metaphor parable, I used the tale style, which includes an introductory question for which the story is the answer. This way the doctrine of the incarnation is laid side by side with the concluding story, the one metaphorically illuminating the other. In a teaching metaphor, I want to control which two subjects are identified for comparison. The introductory question could easily be removed, allowing hearers to search for the referent or second subject. With the introductory question removed, the parable might function as a judicial or an example-metaphor parable, depending on what individual hearers identify as the parable's referent to lay side by side with the parable.

Let's double-check that the parable fulfills all seven characteristics of a parable. "The Word Became Flesh" is narrative prose. It is not poetic or symbolic. The story is metaphorical, illuminating in one particular, concrete way how words can become tangible. The parable is brief, using only 220 words. As a spoken piece, the parable can be read in seventy-five seconds. The parable has a teaching function that can be transformative. The story has a twist in that spoken words do literally become flesh through actions. This strange perspective reframes the issue of the tangibility of words. Most people would not have thought about words in this way before allowing the story's conclusion to be surprising. The parable was created with the hearers' context in mind. And, when delivered, the parable will function covertly as the meaning slips into their subconscious providing insight. "The Word Became Flesh" does indeed fulfill the characteristics of parable.

After the parable is in a more or less final form, the mode of delivery has to be chosen. The parable is only a tool, and its effectiveness is determined by how it will be used. In what context will it be used to attempt to transform the audience? When will it be delivered? Who will present it? Will the parable be given in written or spoken form? Will the parable be introduced or will it stand on its own? In this example, "The Word Became Flesh" could be used in a variety of ways. The parable could be a discussion starter for a Bible study. It could be an illustration in a sermon. The parable could be published in the church newsletter. Sunday school teachers might be given copies to use in their classes. The congregation might be given copies to use at home as part of their family Advent devotions. Choosing how the parable is delivered is sometimes as important as the creation of the parable itself. In this example, I used the parable as an illustration in a sermon on John 1:1–18. The parable was effective in helping congregants experience the incarnation in a relational way.

Drifting Outside the Boundaries

Using the seven characteristics of parabolic literature as boundary markers, writers are able to create transformative literature that makes a difference in the world. But, these seven characteristics are only blurry boundary markers, and every literary rule is more a guideline than an inflexible law. There are no literary police who will arrest parable writers for crossing the nebulous line. However, parable writers who stray too far from the defining boundary markers risk having their work become ineffective as parables the more their work draws closer to other genres of literature.

While parables are generally brief, there is not a specific word count where a story leaves being a parable and becomes a short story or novella. A few parables have been published as book-length stories. *Who Moved My Cheese?* by Spencer Johnson is one example.[2] But this should be considered an exception rather than the norm. Other parables can be quite effective when told only with a single sentence. Jesus's parable of the mustard seed is a tale-style parable composed of only a single sentence just fifty-four words long. But in that single sentence, the story still has a beginning, middle, and end. Plot is not sacrificed in the brevity of its telling. Generally, writing *shorter* parables is more difficult than writing longer ones. A well-written short parable is often more difficult to create than a story ten times the parable's length.

Because parables are brief, details must be left out of the story. The observation has already been made that there is virtually no description in the earlier parable, "Smacked in the Head with a Shovel." The meaning is found only in the action. Description only distracts from the intended point. When details or descriptions are added to a parable, there should be a purpose for their inclusion. For instance, in "The Lost Penny" there are two characters, Tom and Tom's uncle. Tom's uncle remains unnamed. He remains unnamed for two subtle reasons. First, naming the nephew makes him more personable. The author is subtly encouraging hearer identification with him over the uncle. Second, the rich uncle who is concerned about money is left impersonally without a name as befits his own impersonal interest in wealth over meaning in life. If writers lengthen a parable by adding description, care should be taken that the length itself does not distract from the parabolic meaning of the story. Because parables are designed to be brief, every word should be chosen to fulfill a specific purpose.

The Subtleties of Context in Using Parables

The two contexts in which a parable lives have already been discussed, but the importance of understanding them cannot be emphasized enough. Hearers must be intimately familiar with metaphors chosen for parables. To slip past the cognitive mind and influence the subconscious, the metaphor has to stir memories and emotions that are already present in the hearer. Nathan could have told King David a story about a wealthy potter and a poor one, but he chose instead to use shepherds in his story. Intellectually, David would have been able to understand the justice issues involved in a story about an abused potter, but he was able to personally experience the story about an abused shepherd.

Nathan called upon his knowledge of David's former occupation as a shepherd to shape the primary metaphor for his parable. The difference between cute little stories and parables that transform is the ability of parable tellers to penetrate hearers' hearts by their choice of metaphors.

These same contextual issues are at stake when a teacher selects a specific parable from a collection for use in a particular teaching context. The most brilliant parable will not connect if the students are unfamiliar with the parable's primary metaphor. For instance, a metaphor that involves milking a cow by hand will probably not connect with urban children. The teacher might be able to explain the concept to the point that students *intellectually* understand it, but they probably won't be *moved* by it. When using parables in mixed audiences, parable tellers must also recognize that not everyone in the group is likely to get the intended point. Parable tellers must then decide whether to use a metaphor that reaches the majority of the people or to target a subgroup within the whole.

Other Considerations in Writing Parables

Because parables work well when there is a disparity of power between the parable teller and the hearer, parables are excellent choices for teaching when that disparity creates problems. Students with authority issues can be reached with parabolic teaching when other methods fail. By using a parable to make a point, the teacher is relinquishing her authority to the characters in the parable. The teacher hears the story in the same way as the students do, and she is free to feign ignorance of the parable's meaning while the students discuss the lessons that can be gleaned from the story. The teacher allows the characters in the parable to be the teacher.

Those who undertake the task of seeking to transform others should examine their own willingness to be transformed. Few things are more pathetic than to see the tables turned and the parable teller have his own issues thrown back in his face because he is resistant to changing himself. Those who open the door by wanting to change others but are unwilling to change themselves not only do not model what they strive to accomplish in others, but become stumbling blocks and even laughingstocks. Opening the door to change in others can backfire when those others want to walk back through the door and demand change in the parable teller. Those who undertake the holy task of transforming others should count the cost of doing so and have taken a careful account of their *own* faults and willingness to change. Jesus made the same point when he taught, "Why do you see the speck in your neighbor's eye, but do not notice the log in your own eye? Or how can you say to your neighbor, 'Let me take the speck out of your eye' while the log is in your own eye? You hypocrite, first take the log out of your own eye, and then you will see clearly to take the speck out of your neighbor's eye" (Matt 7:3–5).

Furthermore, motivation for telling a parable is important. Particularly within religious contexts, what kind of transformation are you seeking to inspire? Within Islam there is a dervish tradition in which clerics present their morally uplifting teachings in parable form to make them more accessible, but dervishes use parables to obscure their teachings more completely. The cleric desires to teach a moral and wants everyone to understand according to their own ability, but the dervish provides enlightenment only to those who try to understand, for it is in the expended effort to understand that parables gain the power to transform hearers.[3] When writing parables, do you intend to teach a moral or to obscure a truth that can only be received with expended effort on the part of hearers? Both methods have value. However, the approach used will be different for each.

Dealing with Failure

When a parable is effective in its intended purpose, there is no greater joy than to bask in the satisfaction that a piece of art you have created has influenced or changed someone else. Likewise the failure of your art to have its planned effect is disappointing. Keep in mind that some parables have a delayed effect and there still might be a time in the future when the parable will break through to the targeted audience. Do not take the failure personally. Parables were *never* intended to be the first line of communication, but a covert way of delivering difficult or unpleasant messages. While a particular parable might not have the effect you desired, it might have functioned in a different way that still had meaning for the intended audience. At the very least the parable was a briefly entertaining distraction in an otherwise busy world. Also, parables have the opportunity to influence secondary audiences when they are shared or published. Remember that the failure of one parable with an intended audience is only the failure of one tactic in a continuing struggle. There will be other opportunities to lobby for transformation.

One afternoon the wise Sufi said to his disciples, "There are jewels everywhere. Why are you not collecting them?"

The disciples began to search, but no one found a single gem. "We don't see any jewels," they said.

The Sufi answered, "Serve! Serve! That is what I mean!"[1]

10.

MODERN PARABLES IN PREACHING AND TEACHING

The Parabolic Preaching Method

The Parable of Truth

The kingdom of God is like a fragment of truth given to four people. The philosopher studies the truth, declares that it really isn't genuine, and discards it. Proud of her effort, the philosopher waits for other expressions of truth, so she might void them too. The lawyer examines the truth carefully and concludes this piece of truth does not apply to him. But he is sure the truth applies to others, so he zealously hurries to court to have others found guilty of breaking it. The economist scrutinizes the truth and finds it totally unprofitable. Since it can't be sold at a profit, merchants won't carry it. The economist concludes the truth is unsalable and worthless. But, the preacher received the truth, loved it, and taught it to her whole congregation. The truth made her very happy. Let anyone with ears to hear listen!

The preaching task is about communicating God's truth to people so it becomes real and useful to them. Not all people are eager to hear that truth. Not all people perceive God's truth as good news. The preaching task is to help people overcome obstacles they have placed in the way of hearing God's truth so they may have an encounter with the divine. Preaching is as much about packaging God's truth in a useful way as it is about espousing it. The latter is the ideal for a congregation that is eager to encounter God. The former is usually more necessary in practice.

Parabolic preaching starts with the congregation. What are their needs and problems for which they are seeking answers? Once the problems have been identified, the preacher develops a plan to present possible solutions to the congregation. A scripture passage is sought that sheds insight on the problem. A parable is developed that provides a metaphorical solution to the problem. Then, the sermon is crafted so that the scripture and the parable provide two different metaphorical solutions to the congregation's presenting problem. If the process is done with integrity, a scripture passage is chosen that truly speaks to the issue. *Isogesis* is forcing a meaning on a passage that does not have that meaning. Parabolic preaching disapproves of isogesis as much as expository preaching does. However, a preacher can go searching for a passage that delivers that meaning without being guilty of isogesis. Tangential meanings of texts can be explored to deliver God's truth with integrity as well.

Integrity in the preaching process comes from within the preacher, not from a particular method chosen for crafting a sermon. Expository preachers who lean so heavily on lectionary aids that they read someone else's interpretation of the text, borrow another person's sermon outline, and fill in that outline with someone else's sappy illustrations without putting anything from themselves into the sermon process do not have integrity. The problem is not with the method, but with the preacher who is too lazy to struggle with the text and the context in which the sermon will be preached. All preachers borrow illustrations and even adapt other preacher's outlines. But when borrowed material is personally shaped and repackaged for the preacher's own congregation, then God's truth gets delivered in a way that transforms the congregation into the body of Christ. While the parabolic preaching method starts with the congregation instead of the biblical text, this method still can be used with integrity.

In the parabolic preaching method, the goal is to throw three things side by side for comparison.

1. A passage of scripture
2. A modern parable
3. The life situations of the hearers

When these three are laid out side by side, hearers can metaphorically compare the three and gain insight. The biblical text and the modern parable both shed insight into hearers' life situations (see Figure 3).

FIGURE 3. Three-Way Metaphorical Comparison

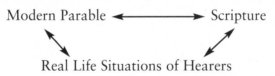

Modern Parable ←————→ Scripture

Real Life Situations of Hearers

A typical outline for a parabolic sermon is as follows:

I. Scripture Reading

II. Sermon

A. Parable

1. Tell a modern parable.

2. Refrain from explaining the parable.

B. Scripture

1. Transition back to the scripture.

2. Explain difficult parts of the scripture.

3. Relate possible meanings of the scripture.

4. Relate the meaning of scripture to the parable.

C. Modern Problem Situation

1. Describe a modern problem.

2. Describe the relevance of the problem to the congregation.

3. Explain how the meaning of the scripture provides a solution to the problem.

D. Parable

1. Refer back to the problems in the parable and show the connections.

2. Refrain from overly explaining the parable.

The parable is an integral part of the sermon. It is not a cute illustration, but a metaphorical part of the whole. Along with the scripture, the parable provides another window into solving the presenting problem.

The following sermon roughly follows the above outline and gives an example of the parabolic preaching style. The presenting problem is helping the congregation sort out the relationships between pleasure, wealth, and happiness. Too many middle-class people believe that more wealth will lead to more happiness in a linear fashion. This sermon is designed to help them call into question the supposed linear relationship between wealth and happiness just as the preacher of Ecclesiastes called this relationship into question long ago. The opening parable is an unfinished tale that closes with a question. After the question is asked, the sermon moves quickly into interpreting the meaning of three related scripture passages in Ecclesiastes. After the meaning has been extracted, it is applied to the characters in the parable. The sermon concludes by asking the congregation how they will answer the question for themselves. The opening parable is more than a cute story; it is integral to the whole sermon. The sermon would be lacking something substantial if the parable were cut out.

Finding the Boundaries of Pleasure

Sermon Texts: Ecclesiastes 2:1–11, 24–26, and 5:8–20.

Once upon a time there were three brothers. The oldest brother was a hard worker. He worked nights to put himself through law school, and upon graduation landed a lucrative job in a prestigious law firm. He worked sixty-hour weeks and amassed a small fortune. He was respected in the community and was known as one of the best lawyers in the state.

The youngest brother married a very wealthy woman. They took frequent trips abroad. They held extravagant parties and ate the finest foods. He and his wife denied themselves nothing. Often they laughed and enjoyed the pleasures money could buy.

The middle brother dropped out of school and became a janitor. He worked hard to support his wife and three children and was known in the community as a family man who enjoyed fishing. On his day off he could often be found at the local lake fishing with his children.

The oldest and youngest sons used to badger their middle brother about his poverty. They continually hassled him, encouraging him to find a more lucrative occupation. They bragged about their wealth, and despised their middle brother for having such low goals in life. But, the oldest brother had a stress-induced stroke at the age of fifty-five. The wealth he had amassed was just enough to cover his medical bills and nursing home care for the rest of his life. The youngest brother, never having had to work a single day in his life, became exceedingly obese. At the age of forty-five he suffered a heart attack and died. The middle brother continued to work and fish and enjoy his grandchildren and great-grandchildren until he died in his sleep at the age of eighty-five. Which of the three brothers really knew what it was like to experience pleasure?

The oldest brother had gained respect and renown in his chosen profession. He derived his pleasure from working hard. The youngest brother had the money to do or buy anything he could ever want. He gained his pleasure from satisfying every desire he had. The middle brother found his enjoyment with his family. These three are not uncommon choices. Many people work exceedingly hard. Many people who have money spend much of it for their enjoyment. Others find pleasure in being with their families. Psychologists today would say that one cannot choose one of the three lifestyles as being better than the others. Whichever lifestyle one prefers is the one that is best for the individual doing the choosing. Perhaps.

The preacher of Ecclesiastes also pondered the question, "What is pleasure?" He asked, "For who knows what is good for mortals while they live the few days of their vain life, which they pass like a shadow? For who can tell them what will be after them under the sun?" (Eccl 6:12). But the preacher asked the question of pleasure in the context of the meaning of life. The preacher was concerned about identifying the boundaries of enjoyment that would allow the individual to be happy while still satisfying the God who would preside at the great judgment following death. The preacher was concerned that if pleasure did not provide meaning in itself, then what was God's purpose for pleasure, and how was one to respond to the many people who could not seem to find pleasure?

In Ecclesiastes 2 the preacher undertook his first great experiment, "I will make a test of pleasure. I will enjoy myself." And, throughout the first ten verses he reported all the activities he had engaged in to test the value of pleasure. He had built gardens and buildings, vineyards and pools. He bought slaves and flocks, silver and entertainers. He fulfilled his appetite with wine, women, and song. He kept no earthly experience from himself. And yet he did not find meaning in his pleasure. Sheer extravagance and self-indulgence were understood by him to be fleeting. They were empty. When one was done with the sensual pleasure, there was no lasting satisfaction that made the preacher feel worthwhile. And, after his great experiment, he had to conclude that there was more to life than seeking after pleasure. Meaning had to come from God. No lasting satisfaction could come from life apart from the God who had given life to begin with.

The impressive extent of the preacher's self-indulgence is reminiscent of the wealth and power of King Solomon, who was probably the richest and most extravagant of all the kings of Israel. The book of Ecclesiastes has traditionally been attributed to Solomon because of the allusions to wealth and wisdom. However, except for the opening verse of the book, which identifies the author as "the Son of David, king in Jerusalem," and the allusions to vast wealth and wisdom throughout chapter 2, there is nothing in the rest of the book that would suggest a royal identity for the author. As a matter of fact, the advice and observations the preacher gives in chapters 4, 8, 9, and 10 on dealing with the king would suggest anything *but* a royal identity for the preacher. Yet, the account of the preacher's test of pleasure found in chapter 2 *is* consistent with what we know about King Solomon, and even though it is probably unlikely that King Solomon wrote Ecclesiastes himself, one can safely assume that the content of chapter 2 is modeled after King Solomon's oral testimony, which probably had been passed down through the sages for generations. And I would also assume that the preacher of Ecclesiastes had probably also made his own test of pleasure, but on a much smaller scale than what was actually described in chapter 2. That the book of Ecclesiastes was probably written by a sage in about the year 200 BCE does not make it any less authentic or valuable for our instruction. The sage is writing his observations on life in the spirit of Solomon's earlier efforts, and, for the year 200 BCE, the sage had a unique message to share.

In the later part of chapter 5 the preacher of Ecclesiastes offered his observations on the relationship between wealth and pleasure. Verses 8 and 9 are problematic verses because the Hebrew syntax of verse 9 is uncertain. But, even with the uncertainties in the text, the verses seem to say that in a world where things are valued, people strive to gain mastery over them. "A plowed field has a king." Someone will seek to gain mastery over the plowed field, and others will seek to gain mastery over that one. And, someone else will seek to gain mastery over the master. Injustice often occurs in this process. The poorer people are, the more likely they will be treated unjustly by those who seek power and privilege. Being poor is not a stated goal of the preacher because of the injustice that often occurs to the poor.

However, in verses 10 and 11, the preacher stated that the opposite of poverty was an equally unwanted state. He wrote, "The lover of money will not be satisfied with money; nor the lover of wealth, with gain....When goods increase, those who eat them increase; and what gain has their owner but to see them with his eyes?" While being poor is not to be highly desired, being rich is not to be highly desired either. In the extremes of wealth and poverty there is unhappiness. Then in verse 12, the preacher lifted up the life of the common worker who is neither rich nor poor. The laborer has food to eat, but must work hard to provide this food. Of the laborer, the preacher wrote, "Sweet is the sleep of laborers, whether they eat little or much; but the surfeit of the rich will not let them sleep." For the preacher, finding peace at the end of each day was important. The poor go to bed hungry and cannot sleep. The rich go to bed with indigestion and cannot sleep. But, the middle class, the ones who have to work hard, they find peace and sleep at the end of each day. The laborers are the ones to be admired.

As in our society today, so also in 200 BCE, wealth and pleasure were often spoken of together. A common perception is that those who have wealth may buy or do whatever they like in order to gain pleasure for themselves. But the preacher is not quick to admit that wealth will bring pleasure, nor will he say that the wealthy always experience pleasure. He also wrote, "There is a grievous ill that I have seen under the sun: riches were kept by their owners to their hurt." Rather than finding pleasure in wealth itself, the preacher of Ecclesiastes asserted that those who truly experience pleasure in this life do so from having gained the pleasure from satisfaction with their current state of affairs. Whether they be poor, middle class, or wealthy, if they are *satisfied*, they have the possibility of experiencing peace and satisfaction. *For the preacher, peace and satisfaction with one's life seemed to be the only true form of pleasure.* But, the preacher asserted, it is harder for the very poor and the very wealthy to find this peace.

The conclusion of the wealth/pleasure issue in chapter 5 is almost identical to the conclusion he drew in chapter 2 after his elaborate test of pleasure. His stated conclusion is as follows, "This is what I have seen to be good: it is fitting to eat and drink and find enjoyment in all the toil with which one toils under the sun the few days of the life God gives us; for this is our lot. Likewise all to whom God gives wealth and possessions and whom he enables to enjoy them, and to accept their lot and find enjoyment in their toil—this is the gift of God."

Of the three brothers—the lawyer, the janitor, and the playboy—the preacher of Ecclesiastes would say that only the janitor experienced pleasure. Seeking wealth and status as the lawyer did gives rise to a lust of false pleasure that can never be satisfied, hence the lawyer's stress-induced stroke at the age of fifty-five. While he was striving after the wind throughout his law career, he probably never experienced true peace and satisfaction with his state of affairs. He always wanted more. The youngest brother who sought to satisfy his sensual appetite, in the preacher's view, likewise failed to find true satisfaction in life. True peace cannot be found through the appeasement of the body's sensual desires. That he died hopelessly overweight is a symptom of his lack of satisfaction with the life of pleasure he led. Only the middle brother, the janitor who liked to fish, found true satisfaction and pleasure in life. Because he was content with his life, the middle brother was able to find peace and joy in the simple life God had given him.

The road to happiness is that of our own choosing. We make choices about the kind of pleasure we seek. But, if we follow the preacher's advice, we must always remember that all pleasure does not lead to happiness. All pleasure does not give meaning in the end. To find true pleasure, we must purposefully set boundaries on our pleasure, so we can find contentment in the lives we already lead. Being too wealthy or too poor are snares on the road to contentment. In the end, finding peace with ourselves and with our God are the only true sources of everlasting pleasure in our lives.

Amen and Amen.

Pitfalls to Avoid in Using Modern Parables in Sermons

Preachers are familiar with illustrations. Illustrations are stories, quotes, or jokes that describe the issue being discussed. They provide color and make topics more memorable. If the illustration was cut out of the sermon, the sermon would still stand, though it might be a bit more boring. Illustrations are usually sought on the basis of their ability to demonstrate a given concept. They are selected after the preacher has outlined the whole. Parables, on the other hand, are integral to the complete structure of a sermon in the parabolic preaching style. The parable is selected at the beginning of the process and the outline of the sermon is wrapped around the parable. If the parable were removed, the sermon would not be complete. When parables are used only as illustrations, the parabolic preaching method is not being used.

Since parables tend to be more powerful than illustrations, preachers should avoid using more than one parable in any given sermon. Preachers want the parable, along with the scripture, to be thrown next to the congregation's life situation. If too many parables are used in a given setting, hearers become distracted and don't make the intended comparison. When I read parables in a collection, I can rarely read more than one at a time. I read the parable and need to close the book and let that parable bounce around my subconscious for awhile. The preacher can control what hearers take away from a given sermon by limiting the material to exactly what should be laid out side by side for comparison. Most of the time in preaching, "less is more."

There is a style of preaching that my wife calls "Nail Sermons." She imagines that preachers start on Monday with a theme for the upcoming sermon on Sunday. For example, the theme might be "love." All week the preacher collects stories and illustrations about love for use in that sermon. The preacher might stick each story on the nail of a desktop memo collector. Each story about love is stuck on the nail on top of the last. Finally, on Sunday, the preacher takes the nail with the collected stories into the pulpit. He reads the scripture, announces the love theme, and then pulls each note off the nail sequentially and reads it without any thought to organizing the illustrations. Each story may go with the theme for the sermon, but in the end, the sermon doesn't have a point. Therefore, a "Nail Sermon" is a pointless thematic sermon with lots of cute stories.

Avoid stringing several parables together when preaching. Parables are too powerful to be used in "Nail Sermons." If the preacher finds several parables that elucidate a particular theme, rather than using them all in the same sermon, a series of sermons can be preached instead. For instance, love is such a broad theme that a preacher who found several parables about it could take each one sequentially and develop a series of sermons that explored different dimensions of love. As a farmer once said to a young pastor who had just preached a particularly long sermon, "You didn't have to give us the whole load." That "load" can be distributed over several sermons. Again, *packaging* is an important part of the preaching task. Finding a manageable lesson for the time provided is critical to preaching with integrity. A congregation can only listen as long as their seat is comfortable. When the congregation starts to fidget, the preacher's effectiveness declines markedly.

When using parables, care should be taken not to overexplain them. Preachers should strive to have the parable make the point. Never explain what the parable means before telling the parable. That is like telling the punch line of a joke before telling the joke. Explaining what the preacher wants the hearer to get out of a parable before the parable is told robs the parable of its ability to slip past the hearer's subconscious. If hearers understand too quickly the preacher's motivation, they may put up their guards and listen to the cute, if not puzzling, story without allowing the parable an opportunity to transform them. Even after the parable is told, I normally try not to explain the parable in detail. I may make some sweeping statements about the gist of the meaning, but I want the hearers to struggle with the meaning themselves. If I explain the parable, it tends to be in relation to the meaning of the scripture. I prefer to explain the scripture in detail and relate the lesson of the scripture back to the parable. When addressing the modern problem faced by the congregation, I will refer back to the similar problems in the parable. I want to lead the congregation so they will know what I want them to compare. I want them to lay the parable, the meaning of scripture, and their personal problems all out side by side. If I am able to do that, then I let the metaphorical processes in their subconscious take over from there and consider the preaching event to be a success.

If a parable is selected from a collection for use in a parabolic sermon, do not include any concluding proverb that might be attached to the parable. The concluding proverb will allow the congregation to make the leap to the parable's meaning too quickly. Rather, make them do their own work by comparing the parable to the scripture and their own life situations and allow them to draw that meaning out for themselves. The temptation is always there to use the concluding proverb. If a preacher must include it, then save it for the end of the sermon. Most of the time, if the scriptures are explained properly, the concluding proverb is unnecessary.

Matching Forms and Genres

The metaphorical comparisons between a parable and a scripture passage are strengthened when the form of the parable matches the form of the scripture. For instance, Mark is famous for his "sandwich" style of storytelling where he interrupts a story in progress to tell another story before finishing the first. The healing of Jairus's daughter (Mark 5:21–24, 35–43) is an example. This story is interrupted by the healing of the woman with the flow of blood (Mark 5:25–34). Mark uses this sandwich technique enough so that it is not accidental but a form of storytelling that he enjoys. Two different formats for healing are compared in Mark's sandwich story, which is more powerful than if the two stories were told sequentially. A parable that is modeled on this form could be developed that told a story within a story. Hearers of the parable and the scripture then have a new appreciation for the message conveyed by the form. Likewise, acrostic passages can be matched with acrostic parables. Dirges can be matched with parables that end unhappily. Visionary scriptures can be matched with parables about dreams. Meaning is often conveyed in form, and helping hearers access that form makes the scriptures come alive.

Authoritarian passages, proverbs, or law passages lend themselves well to being explored with parables that use exaggeration or literalism. Preachers start with the scripture and ask, "What if we were to take this law or teaching to its logical extreme?" For instance, take Matthew 5:29 as an example: "If your right eye causes you to sin, tear it out and throw it away; it is better for you to lose one of your members than for your whole body to be thrown into hell." A parable might be developed about a wounded man who started slicing off body parts to avoid sin and the logical consequences of such behavior. Using exaggeration to explore the limits of taking Jesus's teaching literally helps the congregation rethink the whole concept of the importance of avoiding sin.

Parables are great for reframing situations. Often scripture passages have been heard so often that they have lost their meaning in the hearts of hearers. Using parables to reframe the meaning of a particular scripture gives that scripture a new life in the hearts and minds of those who are able to see it from a new perspective because of contact with a parable. Parabolic preaching gives congregations a new window from which to see scripture, and it gives preachers another tool in the preaching toolbox. Armchair philosophers, lawyers, and economists in the congregation might be coaxed into seeing God's truth from a different perspective because of a parable's ability to reframe that truth in a more useful way for them. Hopefully, they will embrace that truth with joy.

A parable is a short narrative fiction. To properly interpret a para-ble, we must pay careful attention to the story. The power of the story is its ability to release and empower the imagination. In story we can re-imagine the world, we can be other than we normally are. But stories can work in one of two ways—they can either support the world as defined and perceived by the dominant culture, or they can subvert that world. The maintenance of the status quo is the func-tion of myth; Jesus' parables belong to the later type of story.

Bernard Brandon Scott[1]

11.

JESUS'S PARABLES IN PREACHING AND TEACHING

Jesus's parables have been read, discussed, interpreted, and preached in Christian communities for nearly two thousand years. Because parables work metaphorically, preachers have been able to throw Jesus's parables alongside the life situations of their parishioners in all ages so that the parishioners were able to make life-changing comparisons. The preaching task always has to be done with humility, realizing that the preacher's goal is not to draw attention to self, but to make the scriptures accessible to the people. Preaching is always dependent on the contexts of the people who will be hearing the message. A brilliant sermon preached in one congregation with great effect will flop in another where the people cannot find a comparison in the para-ble to illuminate their own situations. Therefore the secret to preaching Jesus's parables is to find something in the parable that will connect with the congregation and preach to emphasize that connection.

There are a variety of ways Jesus's parables can be preached effectively with integrity. In fact, variety in preaching is always a good thing. Preachers who get stuck in a rut and preach every text with the same formula become boring for the parishioner who comes every Sunday. Furthermore, some people are visual learners, others auditory learners, and still others are kinesthetic in their approach to new information. Visual learners love when the preacher uses visual aids to assist the sermon. Auditory learners are already in the zone, since preaching is an auditory activity. Kinesthetic learners use emotion and motion as their preferred method of acquiring information. Sermon activities and preaching that sparks emotion are helpful for them. I once created a giant board game out of paneling and used it for a sermon series on the seven deadly sins. The kinesthetic learners actually enjoyed playing the game after worship each Sunday during the series. Preachers that incorporate a variety of styles and forms in their preaching are more likely to speak to every parishioner over the long haul.

Preaching is a lot like cooking. Those who pull their chair up to the table will enjoy their favorite dishes and eat a few meals they don't particularly like, but over the long haul they will get good nutrition if they clean their plates each time. Not every parishioner will like every sermon, but the hope is they will receive spiritual nourishment if they continue to show up and listen. Variety is important in cooking as well as in preaching.

This chapter explores three approaches for preaching Jesus's parables for the twenty-first century. There are certainly many more ways Jesus's parables can be preached, but these three methods provide some variety. First, Jesus's parables can be retold in story fashion with a modern context. Second, the historical-critical approach to biblical scholarship can be used to dissect a parable for explanation. And third, a moral can be distilled from one of Jesus's parables and preached as the thesis statement of the sermon. Each of these three approaches will be described, followed by an example sermon.

Retelling Jesus's Parable with a Modern Context

Jesus's parables can be retold using a modern context. The retelling needs to be done with some creativity. If the original parable is simply updated without respect to the cultural differences between the original audience and a modern audience, the result is often laughable but ineffective. Take for instance the parable of the ten maidens from Matthew 25:1–13. If the story is simply modernized by having ten young women bring flashlights but no extra batteries, the resulting story is strange from a twenty-first-century American perspective. There is no twenty-first-century tradition of having bridesmaids wait at the reception hall with flashlights. The modernized version has failed to take into account the difference in wedding traditions between the first and twenty-first centuries. If the theme of being prepared after an unexpected wait is to be chosen as the theme for a modern parable loosely based on Matthew 25:1–13, then perhaps a story can be told about ten young women who were waiting by the limousine outside the church ready to shower the bride and groom with birdseed, or to fill the air with soap bubbles, as the newlyweds were to leave for the reception hall. However, the bride and groom were delayed taking pictures after the ceremony and the ten young women were forced to wait in the hot June sun for a much longer time than expected. The parable can describe how each young woman spent her time, either wisely or foolishly, and how the bride and groom reacted to the situation when they suddenly came out. The goal of the preacher is *not* to rewrite scripture. The goal is to tell a related story that helps the congregation better understand the scriptural parable. As such, the preacher should avoid claiming the related story is improved, better than, or an updated version of scripture. Rather, the new parable is simply a *similar* story to the scripture, but should *never* be understood as an attempt to *replace* the scripture.

The modern parable normally should be told at the beginning of the sermon without any introduction. After it has been told, some words of explanation about the scriptural parable can be delivered. The hope is that the congregation will make the metaphorical connection between the two before the preacher has to explain the connection. Once the metaphorical comparison is realized, the subconscious metaphorical process begins to work and the preaching event is successful. Here is an example sermon.

Being Shrewd

Sermon Texts: Proverbs 28:8, 16; Luke 16:1–13.

The Parable of the Conniving Bookkeeper

There was a head bookkeeper of a Fortune 500 company, that with the knowledge of the company's CEO, cooked the books to hide a short-term financial loss so that the CEO would be able to collect a large financial incentive payout to upper executives for the company remaining profitable. As it happened, in a completely unrelated turn of events, there was a middle-level executive in the advertising department who was jealous that the head bookkeeper had an office with a bigger window than he had. So, he made allegations to the CEO, anonymously of course, that the head bookkeeper had been guilty of pilfering office supplies. The CEO confronted the head bookkeeper and told him to clean out his desk, for he was to be terminated at the end of the day.

The head bookkeeper laid his head on his desk and cried. He knew that he would never be able to get a job as good as he had it now. He had alimony and Mercedes Benz payments to make and didn't want to go back to driving a Chevy, so he concocted a plan to keep his job. He called the SEC and reported irregularities in the company's bookkeeping practice. Then he quickly uncooked the books, making it look like the previous report was a mistake caused by a faulty computer program. The blame for the mistake would be born by an outside computer consultant. The corrected statement would reveal the true loss of profit within the company and the CEO would have to give back the financial incentive payout he had already received.

When the CEO first received the phone call from the SEC, thoughts of going to jail under President Bush's new corporate reform bill entered his mind. Terrified, he immediately went to the head bookkeeper to check on damage control. The head bookkeeper explained the efforts he had made to get the CEO into trouble and then back out of trouble again. Instead of being furiously angry with the head bookkeeper because he would have to give back his financial incentive, the CEO laughed and congratulated the head bookkeeper on his shrewdness. The bookkeeper would be reinstated to his old job after all.

For centuries Bible scholars have struggled with the meaning of Jesus's parable of the dishonest manager. Everyone seems to agree that the manager in the story is acting dishonestly, but nobody can come up with a particularly good reason why the boss praises him for being a cheat. The parable is embarrassing, not only because the bad guy gets away with it, but because the bad guy is praised for being dishonest! Luke seems to have struggled with the meaning of this parable too because he tacks on no less than three moralizing endings for his audience to pick from. First, children of the light should be as shrewd as the worldly. Second, we must use crooked cash faithfully to ensure "eternal housing." And, third, we must be faithful with cash in order to be trusted with more cash.[2] Unfortunately, none of these morals are very satisfying. There must be some piece of information we are missing in order to interpret the story properly.

Based on his studies of first-century banking practices, William Herzog has made a case for a different interpretation of the parable of the dishonest manager.[3] If he is right, then the story I just told about the head bookkeeper and the CEO would be a very close modern equivalent. As it turns out, Jesus's ancient parable is particularly relevant in our modern age of cooked books and corporate greed.

Knowing a few details about first-century banking practices helps Jesus's parable truly make sense. The Hebrew Bible forbade the collecting of interest on a loan. There were no exceptions. Collecting *any* interest was considered usurious and prohibited by

Jewish law. However, there has always been a need for loans. The poor often needed loans to get them through hard times, and the rich always had excess capital at their disposal. There were shady banking practices in place that helped bankers get around the usury laws. In the first century, one popular way was not to report the amount of money borrowed, but only to report the amount of money to be repaid. Interest was never mentioned in the payment agreement, even though the repayment amount was always larger than the amount borrowed. If the high priest ever inspected the records looking for the crime of usury, the banking records only showed what each borrower owed and when the money was due.

Frequently, loans were made with commodities instead of cash. Often the commodities were borrowed from estate managers who oversaw the estates of the wealthy instead of borrowing from an established bank. Each commodity had a different hidden interest rate. Olive oil, for instance, spoiled more easily than wheat. Therefore, the interest rate on olive oil was 50 percent, while the interest rate on wheat was only 20 percent. The estate manager would negotiate the rate and add a hidden fee on top of the transaction that he kept for himself. There were no disclosure laws, so the uneducated peasant farmers had no idea just how badly they were being cheated.

A typical transaction is actually described within the parable itself. A peasant farmer who needed to borrow eighty containers of wheat would do so at 20 percent interest. One year later he would owe the original eighty containers *plus* an additional sixteen containers of wheat that represented the interest. The estate manager would add on his fee of, say, four containers of wheat for setting up the transaction. Therefore, at the end of one year that peasant farmer would be required to pay one hundred containers of wheat to the estate manager. Because the loan document would only show the name of the peasant farmer, one hundred containers of wheat, and the due date, the estate manager wouldn't get in trouble for usury.

We are twenty centuries more advanced than the economics of the first century, yet our modern banking systems are just as corrupt! We now have state-mandated maximum limits on the amount of interest that can be charged on a loan, yet there are businesses that specialize in creative accounting. I called a check-cashing company in town this week. I told them I needed to borrow $200 for a couple of weeks. They told me that would be just fine. If I would write them out a check for $234 they would hold it for two weeks before cashing it. They didn't call the $34 extra dollars I would have to pay interest on the loan; they called it a check-cashing fee. When I got out my calculator, the annual interest rate on that two-week loan was 442 percent! Perhaps this is why Jesus also said, "The poor will always be with you." The most vulnerable citizens in our city are paying more than 400 percent interest on their loans! This is an outrage today, just as the collecting of 20 percent or 50 percent interest was an outrage in first-century Palestine.

The manager in Jesus's parable was the broker for the rich man's commodities. The manager kept the books. He made sure the high priest couldn't discern that interest was being collected. He made sure the rich man got his money with interest. And the manager probably took a fee on each transaction. In the parable, the manager was going to be dismissed because the rich man had heard allegations of misconduct. The parable doesn't exactly say that the manager was actually guilty. The rich man accused him, called him to give account, and asserted that he was to be fired. The implication of the story is that the rich man had already made up his mind even though the manager had yet to open the books and defend himself.

Knowing that the future looked bleak, the manager did a very shrewd thing: he called all of the master's debtors one by one and reduced what they had to pay back. The manager did not take the same amount off each person's bill across the board. Rather, the manager reduced each bill by exactly the amount of the interest plus the manager's fee. He reduced each person's bill by exactly the amount that was illegal for him to collect! His final act as steward of the rich man's property was to make the rich man's books legal again.

The parable said that the manager hoped the people might welcome him into their homes. Perhaps they would do so for short-term hospitality, but this was not really a long-term solution for his lack of a job. Estate managers like him were despised by the peasants precisely because he was the person who had the dirty job of announcing the illegal interest rate. By making the books legal again, what the estate manager was really doing was announcing his worth to his employer. The rich man knew that illegal interest was being collected on loans the manager arranged. After the books had been uncooked, the rich man would be able to judge for himself just how much money the manager had made for the rich man.

By reducing the loans by the amount of the illegal interest, the manager was just doing what was legal and right by Jewish law. Therefore, the rich man had no cause for legal complaint. Furthermore, each of the peasants who got the amount of their loan reduced would be grateful, not just to the manager, but also to the rich man for having authorized the reductions. In the eyes of the people, the rich man was transformed into a generous and loving overlord. What he lost in illegal interest would be recouped from the loyalty and gratitude the people would give him in the future. If the rich man fired the manager and reneged on the manager's reductions, there would be an uproar in the village and the rich man would be seen as a villain. One of the disgruntled peasants had probably been the source of the anonymous charges brought against the manager in the first place. Perhaps that peasant would become angry enough so as to complain to the high priest about the rich man's usury. The rich man rightly understood the predicament he was in. Instead of being angry, the rich man congratulated the manager on his shrewdness.

Today, our present society is filled with shady business practices, sweetheart deals, cooked books, and a disdain for the working class and poor. Perhaps one of the messages being communicated by this parable is that it is perfectly acceptable to be honest. When the manager quit charging usurious interest rates, the people were filled with gratitude and he got his job back. Honest businessmen sleep peacefully each night without fear.

In the light of this new information about what was happening in the parable between the lines, we find that there is a basis for all three of Luke's moralizing conclusions. First, when dealing with spiritual matters, Christians should show creativity and shrewdness just as the worldly do when they deal with worldly concerns. Second, those who can't deal honestly with other people's property should not be left to deal with their own. This includes spiritual things as well as earthly. And third, those who are found to be trustworthy in small things can indeed be trusted with more responsibility. Personally, I think the parable is a call to honesty. Be honest in your dealings with others and you will stay out of trouble. I wish the corporate world would take this message to heart. Honesty is still the best policy.

Amen and Amen.

Explaining the First-Century Background of Jesus's Parable

A second approach to preaching Jesus's parables can be found in the historical-critical method of exegesis, which is used to dissect one of Jesus's parables, explaining each part of the parable so hearers can understand what Jesus originally intended. This is a twentieth-century approach to preaching, and as long as it isn't overdone, can be effective in helping hearers understand the original intention of the parable. Care should be taken to apply that original meaning of the scripture to the lives of hearers. Otherwise, the sermon ends up being a lecture or a Bible study instead of a preaching event. A sermon must help the hearers make a comparison of some aspect of their personal lives with Jesus's parable. A Bible study teaches. A sermon also edifies and inspires.

There are many commentaries on Jesus's parables in print, as well as commentaries on the synoptic gospels with accurate and cutting-edge scholarship on the meaning of Jesus's parables. Many of these commentaries do not agree with each other, and the preacher is left to sift through possible interpretations of each parable for the preacher's own congregation. Care should be taken to do this research with integrity. One can always find some obscure author who has written something outlandish on how a particular parable should be interpreted. Preachers should avoid spending time during the preaching event refuting the views of scholars of whom the congregation has never heard. The goal of preaching is not to lead the congregation to view the preacher as particularly brilliant or scholarly. Rather, the goal of the preaching event is to offer the congregation the best scholarship available to help them find a meaning for Jesus's parables that will speak to them in the present.

The following is an example sermon.

The High Cost of Biblical Illiteracy

Sermon Texts: Proverbs 22:22–23; Luke 16:19–31.

There was a father who bought a tree-house kit for his child's eighth birthday. He immediately threw away the instructions. He thought he could figure it out. Into the late hours of the night he worked, but the tree house just wouldn't go together like the picture on the box. He still refused to read the instructions. He hammered and sawed and assembled, and in triumph, he went to bed at two in the morning. The next day his daughter climbed up into the new creation and the floor gave way and she fell ten feet and broke both arms.

There was a woman who wanted to call an old friend, but she didn't want to bother looking the number up in the phone book. She remembered four of the seven numbers. So she started dialing, trying to guess her friend's phone number. She never did get to talk to her friend.

A young student had a very important test to take at school one day. She didn't study the text book but watched television instead. She failed the exam.

An elderly gentleman was driving across the country to attend an army reunion. He refused to take a map. He was sure he could find the place. Even when he became hopelessly lost, he wouldn't stop and ask for directions. He never did get to the reunion, and he was a long time getting back home again.

There was a rich man who wanted to go to heaven after he died and meet God. The rich man was always too busy counting his money or buying a new car or taking a trip and didn't have time to go to church. He was too busy to pray. He didn't read his Bible. He never contributed to charity. He believed that God would roll the red carpet out for him when he died. He was wrong.

Sometimes humans are lazy, and they think they can do something without following the directions or learning how to do it right. Occasionally, they'll get lucky, but most of the time laziness results in disaster. So it is with the spiritual world. People who are lazy about spiritual things will also meet spiritual disaster at the last judgment. The Parable of the Rich Man and Lazarus is primarily a story about just one such spiritual disaster.

The rich man in our New Testament lesson today wasn't completely lazy. He dressed in the finest linen and purple cloth every day. He feasted sumptuously and knew all the latest trends. He wasn't lazy in everything. *He was only lazy when it came to his spiritual life.* He made assumptions about how God would want him to act. And, to be quite honest, he assumed wrong! The story ends in tragedy with him in Hades being tormented by flames of fire. Of course, from the point of view of Lazarus, the story has a very happy ending. Lazarus rests in Abraham's bosom and eats from Abraham's table. Whereas on earth Lazarus ate scraps thrown in the street, he dined sumptuously in the life to come.

The parable doesn't moralize about exactly why Lazarus went to paradise and the rich man went to perdition. The text does not say that Lazarus was righteous or the rich man was wicked. But if we look at the interaction between the two, we can readily discern why each man went to his correct place. The clues to the rich man's wickedness are found in his interactions with both Lazarus and Abraham.

Before his death, the rich man lived in a palace with a gate. The gate is important in the story because the gate symbolizes separation. While the rich man lived in splendor inside the palace, Lazarus lay at the rich man's gate on the other side of the wall. The rich man would not let Lazarus into his house. Lazarus was not a welcome friend in the rich man's home. Likewise, in the afterlife, the chasm kept the rich man from entering Lazarus's home with Abraham. The gate in the story was not only a symbol of exclusion, but also a symbol of justice. Legal decisions were made at the city gates. Public announcements were made at the gate. Lazarus was laying at the rich man's gate and not only was he forbidden entrance but was denied hospitality. Lazarus was treated unjustly.

The story indicates that the rich man knew Lazarus. Lazarus was not just a nameless beggar. Ironically, Jesus told the story without giving the rich man a name. The villain in the story is just a nameless rich man. They are a dime a dozen. The beggar, on the other hand, is afforded the dignity of a name in Jesus's parable. Lazarus's name means "God has helped." While the help might not be readily apparent in his earthly life, certainly in the life to come God helped Lazarus tremendously. The story indicates that the nameless rich man did indeed know who Lazarus was. When the rich man spoke to Abraham, he called Lazarus by name. The rich man knew Lazarus and knew that Lazarus lay at his gate. Furthermore, the rich man knew that Lazarus did not receive any hospitality from him. The rich man knowingly let Lazarus fight with the dogs over table scraps. That the rich man personally knew Lazarus compounds the severity of his lack of hospitality.

In the first century, the rich did not use cloth napkins to wipe their hands after a meal as we do today. They used pieces of leftover bread to wipe their hands. Then, the soiled bread was thrown into the street and the dogs and beggars were allowed to fight over it. Lazarus was in such poor health that he couldn't even fight the dogs well and the dogs took advantage of Lazarus, even licking Lazarus's sores as they both waited for the scraps to be thrown into the street. The rich purposefully soiled the leftover bread from their tables by wiping their hands on them before casting them into the street. With only a slight bit more effort, the rich could have wiped their hands elsewhere and allowed the poor to have clean, fresh bread. The callousness of their actions is shocking.

Furthermore, if we look at the relationship between the rich man and Lazarus, we see that the rich man never addressed Lazarus directly. The rich man asked Abraham to send Lazarus over the chasm to give him a drop of water to quench his thirst. He didn't ask Lazarus personally. The rich man was assuming that the social standing that he enjoyed on earth still applied in the afterlife. He was too important to address a beggar or a common laborer. He went straight to the top and asked Abraham to allow Lazarus to serve him. Even suffering in perdition, the rich man could only think of Lazarus as a servant, a tool to be used and cast aside. The rich man's attitude condemned him. He was a selfish, greedy, abusive man.

The rich man went to perdition, not because he was rich, but because he was an uncaring and heartless cad. Remember that Abraham, himself, was a rich man in his own day. But Abraham was a rich man with ethics and compassion. Abraham allowed Lot to choose the best grazing land for himself. Abraham refused to take spoils of war from the king of Sodom even though Abraham had the right to do so. Abraham bought the cave in which he buried Sarah even though the cave was offered to him free of charge. Abraham was generous and ethical in his dealings with others. Rich people can go to heaven, even though the particular rich man in Jesus's parable did not. As John Stanley Glen put it, "It would be wrong to equate riches with sin and poverty with piety, as suggested by the simple, uninterpreted fact that the rich man went to hell and the beggar to heaven. The impression that the former ended in perdition for no other reason than the fact that he was rich, and that the latter ended in glory for no other reason than the fact that he was poor, is a sociological interpretation the Bible does not sanction....It is not the rich man's wealth but his callous lovelessness and impious self-indulgence that are condemned; similarly, it is Lazarus's humble piety that is commended, not his poverty. Thus the ungodly rich are punished, and the pious poor rewarded."[4] The rich man got where he was by being too lazy to find out what God expected and doing it. The rich man is surprised by his situation. He is ignorant of God's plan for salvation.

This ignorance can clearly be seen as he argues with Abraham about the salvation of his five brothers. Under the guise of caring about what happened to his five brothers, the rich man asked

Abraham to send Lazarus to warn them about perdition. Indirectly, the rich man was really trying to play on Abraham's sympathies. He was trying to show Abraham that his only sin was ignorance. He would have acted more appropriately on earth if he had known better. The realities of the spiritual world were not explained carefully enough so that he could understand. If only Abraham would send a servant, like Lazarus, to his brothers they would change their ways. The rich man was appealing to Abraham's sense of compassion, since Abraham had once pleaded to God on behalf of the wicked residents of Sodom. But Abraham told him that they have Moses and the prophets to warn them. The rich man complained that the Bible is not enough. If only a dramatic messenger from the dead will go and warn them they will listen. Abraham doesn't buy it. The Bible will have to be enough.

In the United States, ignorance of the law is no excuse for breaking the law. My best friend from high school used to be a prosecuting attorney. He used to say that being stupid wasn't a crime. The police can't arrest someone for being stupid. But people *can* be arrested for being ignorant. Breaking a law, even if the person doesn't know about that law, is indeed a crime and is punishable. Likewise, in the spiritual realm, ignorance of God's law does not excuse a person from having to answer to the consequences of breaking it. In the case of the rich man in Jesus's parable, the cost of ignorance was eternal suffering in perdition.

God has chosen to communicate God's message through the Bible. Knowing that, we should have a strong interest and desire to read and study the Bible so we will not be found to be ignorant on the day of judgment. The rich man probably had good intentions. He didn't know that he would be held accountable for his callousness toward Lazarus. If only someone would have told him, he would have repented. Abraham reminded him that he had had Moses and the prophets to teach him.

As humans we tend to assume we can guess how to do stuff. So we tackle putting together tree houses without reading the directions. We take tests without studying. We try to navigate without using a map. And most of the time we meet disaster. The same is true of the spiritual life. If we don't take time to read the instruction book, the Bible, chances are we will also meet disaster. The rich man in the parable wanted to warn someone of the dangers of being ignorant. Consider yourselves warned. Amen and Amen.

Preaching the Moral of Jesus's Parables

A third approach to preaching Jesus's parables involves distilling a moral from one of the parables and preaching the moral. Many of Jesus's parables have multiple valid morals that can be distilled from the parable. The secret to preaching using this method is to know the congregation well enough to preach a moral that is necessary for their continued spiritual growth. Take for instance Jesus's parable of the prodigal son from Luke 15:11–32. The parable is complex enough to draw several valuable morals: Don't waste your inheritance or you'll eat pig slop. Good fathers love their children regardless of their choices. Celebrate repentance with a party. An older brother shouldn't be jealous of his father's love for another sibling. Depending upon the needs of the congregation, one of the morals is selected, which then becomes the thesis statement of the sermon. The sermon is free to draw upon stories and material that support the thesis statement. The scriptural parable is, of course, part of the support for the thesis, but does not have to be the main focus of the sermon. Preachers do need to take care that the parable they choose does support the moral they select.

Most of Jesus's parables lend themselves to a variety of morals. I've even had fun preaching the same text three or four Sundays in a row looking at different aspects of the scripture for that congregation. The scriptures are multifaceted and it promotes spiritual growth to help a congregation see the complexity and versatility of the scriptures for their own lives.

The following is an example sermon.

The Parable of the Tomato Plant: A Sermon

Sermon texts: Daniel 4:10–12; Luke 13:6–9, 18–19.

"I can be a Christian without going to church," the young woman exclaimed.

Her elderly grandfather paused before answering, "Yes, but can you be a *good* Christian without going to church? Let's go out to the garden and pick some tomatoes. I want to show you something."

As they made the short walk from the house, the sun shone down brightly. The young woman went ahead carrying a basket, while the older man limped along with a cane. She was walking along the long row of tomato plants with several large tomatoes already in the basket before he caught up.

"Why do you think some of the tomatoes are larger than others?" he asked.

"I don't know."

"Look the plants over carefully and tell me why some of the tomato plants have predominantly small fruit while other plants have large fruit."

She started looking at the end of the row where a large tree shaded several plants throughout most of the day. "These all have small fruit; I guess because they don't get as much sunlight as they would like."

"Yes, likewise the Christian who does not reach up and bask in God's light will likewise grow small fruit. What else do you notice about the tomato plants?"

"The plants on this other end also have small fruit. They get plenty of sun, but there are a bunch of weeds growing around the plants. Could the weeds cause the plant to produce small tomatoes?"

The older man nodded, "Yes, weeds steal valuable nutrients and force the tomato plant to compete. The result is small tomatoes. Likewise, the Christian who is constantly distracted with evil or unwholesome activities can never be productive. That Christian is choked by the weeds of wickedness.

"There is one more set of plants in the garden that produce small tomatoes. What is wrong with their situation?"

After looking the plants over for a short time she found the plants he intended and observed aloud, "They get plenty of sun. There aren't any weeds. Yet the plants look smaller than the rest and the fruit is very tiny. Could it be soil? There are so many rocks right here."

The older man nodded again. "Yes, good soil is a requirement for big tomatoes. The plants that produce the biggest tomatoes get full sunlight, are free of weeds, and grow in good soil. With a good root system and proper nutrition in the soil, the plant is able to thrive. Likewise, the Christian who is not nurtured and fed in a church community does not have solid roots and can never be very fruitful. The Christians who have the most zeal for mission and have the most compassionate ministries that help others share these three characteristics in common with the tomato plant: they reach for God's light, are free of the weeds of wickedness, and have solid roots in a church community. People can be Christians anywhere, but productive Christians have these traits. What kind of Christian do you want to be? How big will be the fruit you produce if you do not stay grounded in a church community?"

The young woman nodded her understanding.

Both the Old and New Testaments have passages that use the way plants grow as a metaphor for the spiritual life. In Daniel, chapter 4, we see that the tree that grows tall reaching for the heavens with firm roots in the soil is a tree that provides shelter for anyone who comes by. Providing shelter is understood as a good thing. Metaphorically, King Nebuchadnezzar was compared to this large tree. People came to find shelter and protection under his limbs. In Luke 13, the tiny mustard seed grew into a large bush that gave shelter to the birds. Earlier in Luke 13, we find the parable of the fig tree in which the expectations for the fig tree are higher than for the mustard bush or the shade tree. The fig tree is expected to produce large figs. Any fig tree that does not produce fruit is cut down and another fig tree is planted in its place. Through these agriculturally based parables we understand that trees and bushes are useful according to their type, whether it be for shade, shelter, or fruit. When the plant does not live up to its expectations, it is no longer useful and is despised. The spiritual implication for these parables is that any person who does not provide shade, shelter, or fruit in God's garden will likewise be found to be a disappointment.

Looking back at the three prerequisites for a tomato plant to thrive and be productive, let us explore the implications for our own spiritual lives. Christians must seek to live in relationship with God, living in the light of God's love just as plants seek the sunlight. Second, Christians must seek to be free of the weeds of wickedness that choke their productivity. These two aspects of the Christian life are important, but today I want to concentrate on good soil in which the roots of a plant thrive.

A seed is planted in good soil so that it germinates, sends out solid roots, and grows. A person who is not likewise grounded in a community of faith can never have deep roots with which to produce fruit. The church community takes small children and teaches them the faith. The church provides instruction in Bible, ethics, morals, social justice, and theology. Without this solid grounding in the Christian faith, the child is left to wander, get lost, and never be productive for God's kingdom. Christian education is an important part of Christian growth. People who do not make any effort to educate themselves or their children in the ways of Christian faith do so at their own peril.

What are some of the essential aspects of being an educated Christian? First, people have to show up! People who do not make a commitment to attend church school or Bible studies on a weekly basis can't be firmly rooted in the faith. Half of the battle is just showing up. People can't learn if they aren't there. Second, the Bible was meant to be read in community. Yes, people can read and study their Bibles at home, and should indeed do that. But when we read and study the Bible *together,* we are able to discuss the implications of the biblical text for our own situation. Our own selfish views of what we think the text means can be challenged. We benefit from the views of others. We hear alternative ways of understanding the text that add to the richness of

PREACHING PARABLES

the text's meaning. And we decide as a community how the community should respond based upon our understanding of the text. Much fruit grows to maturity when the gathered community makes a decision to act because the community understands the meaning of a particular biblical passage. Third, people have to do their homework. Church school classes and Bible studies often come with study guides that should be read in advance. Christians who come ready to discuss are ready to engage in meaningful study that changes their lives. These three things—showing up, studying in community, and coming prepared—will help Christians be better rooted in faith.

If Christian education represents growth in the Christian life, then worship provides the energy. Worship is *not* a form of entertainment. Worship is the gathered community's expression of praise and gratitude to the God of Heaven and Earth. When Christians lift up their praises in song, confess their sins and find forgiveness, hear the Word read and preached, offer their gifts, and connect with other like-minded Christians, then Christians leave the worship service reenergized and ready to tackle the next week. Worship is supposed to be life giving and renewing. God created humans so that we work best when we participate in worship on a weekly basis. Coming twice a month isn't enough. Would you fail to recharge your cell phone batteries? Would you fail to refill the fuel tank in your car? Would you fail to eat three meals in a day? Refueling and recharging are necessary parts of our lives. Without also recharging our spiritual lives through worship, we burn out, run out of spiritual energy, or become discouraged.

Here are some of the essential aspects for being a worshipful Christian. First, people have to show up! Worship won't recharge people who aren't there. The beauty of the church is that churches are everywhere. If Christians are on vacation, they may be on vacation from work but are not on a vacation from God. They can attend a church close by their motel. Those who have lake homes or visit relatives on weekends can surely find a church to attend. If family comes to visit, they can be brought to church or they can sit by themselves for an hour alone while the faithful

190

Christian does go to church. If Christians have other things they have to get done at home on a Sunday, they should consider the consequences of not recharging their spiritual batteries before skipping church. What else could be skipped instead?

Second, worship requires participation. Worship was never meant to be passive. Television is passive. Worship is dynamic. That means Christians must open their hymnals and sing! They must participate in the unison prayers and responsive readings. They must sort through their sins when confession comes around and offer sincere apology to God. People who claim that church is "boring" also tend to be the people who don't participate as they should. People who aren't actively seeking to connect with God at worship are likely not to be disappointed when they don't find God there. God desires to connect with people who are seeking.

Third, worship is not always about what is best for each individual personally. Worship is about what is best for the community. Adults must be patient while the children are nurtured at the children's sermon. Small children must be patient during the main sermon. If the hymn selection or anthem does not appeal to someone's musical taste that particular day, then they should concentrate on the meaning of the words or seek to try that unfamiliar hymn anyway. People can be fed spiritually and walk away from worship transformed and recharged even when the sermon was boring, the music was dreadful, and the lay leader spoke too softly. Worship is about celebrating God's love in community. These three things (showing up, participating enthusiastically, and being part of community) make worship the weekly event that feeds our roots.

If Christian education represents growth, and worship represents energy, then fellowship and mission provide the vehicles for distributing the fruit. What are some of the signs of life-giving fellowship and mission? First, people have to show up! Fellowship events are about making friends and providing nurturing support for each other. Mission is about distributing the fruit of our love to others. Neither of these duties can be fulfilled unless people show up. Second, people must learn to be tolerant of one another. Jesus didn't say we had to *like* everyone, but he did say we had to *love* everyone. Yes, there are going to be people in the community that are harder to love than others. This just means we get more opportunities to practice the love of God. To be tolerant does not mean we have to agree with everyone or embrace their sins or lifestyles, or even to approve of their choices. Being tolerant means that we voluntarily give up the right to pass judgment and allow God to judge them for their shortcomings while we practice loving them anyway. We should never forget that we have our own sets of shortcomings for which God will judge us. We hope that the rest of the church community will be as tolerant with us as we are with them. Third, fellowship and mission should be fun and meaningful. Sharing our tomato slices in mission and making friends should be rewarding. These three things—showing up, being tolerant of others, and having fun—are part of being rooted in the church community through fellowship and mission.

People desire to have a relationship with God and produce fruit for God's kingdom. There are many elements that go into being fruitful, including seeking to live in God's light, refraining from the weeds of wickedness, and being rooted in the church community of faith. Having strong roots are important to being fruitful. I hope that you will strengthen your roots in this particular church community. And I hope you will be fruitful. Just how big do you want your tomatoes to be?

Amen and Amen.

Hercules and the Wagoner

A wagoner was once driving a heavy load along a very muddy way. At last he came to a part of the road where the wheels sank halfway into the mire, and the more the horses pulled, the deeper sank the wheels. So the wagoner threw down his whip, and knelt down and prayed to Hercules the Strong. "O Hercules, help me in this my hour of distress," quoth he. But Hercules appeared to him, and said:

"Tut, man, don't sprawl there. Get up and put your shoulder to the wheel."

Aesop[1]

12.

FOR FURTHER READING

The Parable of the Armchair Knight

Two men were invited to enter a jousting tournament. Both men had dreamed of being knights, but had no practical experience. Both men ordered the equipment from a catalog: suits of armor, visors, lances, and swords. The first man contracted with a stable to borrow a horse so he could practice jousting. He hung loops on a tall pole and galloped his horse toward the pole trying to penetrate the loop with his lance. He wasn't very good, but he kept on practicing. The second man got a book from the library on jousting and read it in his armchair. The book was fascinating. He learned it all by heart, so he didn't feel a need to practice in preparation for the tournament.

When the day of the tournament came, the first man jousted nobly and earned the respect of the court. The second man fell off his horse before the first pass without his opponent having touched him with a lance. The second man lost the tournament, but from his reading, he knew where he had gone wrong.

Those who want to practice the skills learned in this book may want to spend some time reading parables. A "further reading" list is below, and in the back of this book is an annotated bibliography. Not every book that claims to contain parables does. And, some parables can be found hidden in literature masquerading as short stories. Let the reader beware! Some of these books are out of print—but that does not mean they are unobtainable. Local libraries are often connected to large libraries so that interlibrary loans are relatively routine and quick. Any good local reference librarian can help a reader find treasure. Also, most used bookshops can track down an out-of-print book for a small fee. With an Internet connection, readers can buy out-of-print and in-print books through the mail with a credit card. Any of the plethora of search engines can get you connected with Web sites specializing in out-of-print books.

Concluding Thoughts

Parables are not just for scholars. Historically, parables have been an important literary genre for change and transformation. Because metaphor is such an important component of language, parables should be returned to their high place of using metaphor to inspire and transform. Anyone can use parables to communicate with others. Anyone can write parables. And certainly, anyone can read parables for personal enlightenment. Go forth and let the one who has ears hear! Amen and Amen.

For Further Reading

Aesop's Fables. www.AesopFables.com.
Augustine. *Sermon on the Mount, Harmony of the Gospels,*

Homilies on the Gospels. Nicene and Post-Nicene Fathers. First Series. Vol. 6. Edited by Philip Schaff et al. Translated by R. G. MacMullen. Peabody, MA: Hendrickson Publishers, Inc., 1994.

Bauckham, Richard. "The Parable of the Vine: Rediscovering a Lost Parable of Jesus." *New Testament Studies* 33 (1987): 84–101.

Buttrick, David. *Speaking Parables: A Homiletic Guide.* Louisville, KY: Westminster John Knox Press, 2000.

Buttrick, George. *The Parables of Jesus.* New York: Harper & Brothers Publishers, 1928.

Calvin, John. *Commentary on a Harmony of the Evangelists, Matthew, Mark, and Luke.* Vol. 2. Translated by William Pringle. Grand Rapids, MI: Wm. B. Eerdmans Publishing Company, 1949.

Carnell, Corbins, and Madeleine Boucher. "Parable." *A Dictionary of Biblical Tradition in English Literature.* Edited by David Lyle Jeffrey. Grand Rapids, MI: Eerdmans, 1992.

Coats, George W. "II Samuel 12:1–7a": An Expository Article. *Interpretation* 40 (April 1986): 170–74.

Corless, Roger J. *The Vision of Buddhism: The Space Under the Tree.* New York: Paragon House, 1989.

Crossan, John Dominic. *The Dark Interval: Towards a Theology of Story.* Niles, IL: Argus Communications, 1975.

Dodd, C. H. *The Parables of the Kingdom.* Revised edition. New York: Charles Scribner's Sons, 1961.

Earl, James W. "Prophecy and Parable in Medieval Apocalyptic History." *Religion and Literature* 31 (Spring 1999): 25–45.

Franzmann, M. "The Parable of the Vine in Odes of Solomon 38:17–19? A Response to Richard Bauckham." *New Testament Studies* 35 (1989): 604–8.

Goldsmith, Martin. "Parabolic Preaching in the Context of Islam." *Evangelical Review of Theology* 15 (July 1991): 272–77.

The Gospel of Buddha. Compiled by Paul Carus. Middlesex, UK: Tiger Books International, 1995 (1915).

Herzog, William R., II. *Parables as Subversive Speech: Jesus as Pedagogue of the Oppressed.* Louisville, KY: Westminster/John Knox Press, 1994.

Jeremias, Joachim. *The Parables of Jesus.* Second revised edition. New York: Charles Scribner's Sons, 1972.

Kafka, Franz. *The Complete Stories and Parables.* Edited by Nahum N. Glatzer. New York: Quality Paperback Book Club, 1971.

Lakoff, George, and Mark Johnson. *Metaphors We Live By.* Chicago, IL: The University of Chicago Press, 1980.

Lathem, Edward Connery, ed. *The Poetry of Robert Frost.* New York: Holt, Rinehart and Winston, 1969.

Lindars, Barnabas. "Jotham's Fable: A New Form-Critical Analysis." *Journal of Theological Studies* 24 (October 1973): 355–66.

Macartney, Clarence Edward. *The Parables of the Old Testament.* New York: Fleming H. Revell Company, 1926.

McLaughlin, John L. "The Use of Isaiah 6, 9–10 in the Book of Isaiah." *Biblica* 75 (1994): 1–25.

Meister Eckhart: The Essential Sermons, Commentaries, Treatises, and Defense. The Classics of Western Spirituality: A Library of the Great Spiritual Masters. Editor-in-Chief, Richard J. Payne. Translation and Introduction by Edmund Colledge and Bernard McGinn. Preface by Huston Smith. Mahwah, NJ: Paulist Press, 1981.

Merton, Thomas. *No Man Is an Island.* Garden City, NY: Doubleday & Company, Inc., 1967.

Nahman of Bratslav: The Tales. Translation, Introduction and Commentaries by Arnold J. Band. Mahwah, NJ: Paulist Press, 1978.

Nash, Walter. *The Language of Humour.* English Language Series Title No. 16. Foreword by Randolph Quirk. New York: Longman Inc., 1985.

O'Murchu, Diarmuid. *Quantum Theology.* New York: The Crossroad Publishing Company, 1999 (1997).

Politzer, Heinz. *Franz Kafka: Parable and Paradox.* Revised and expanded edition. Ithaca, NY: Cornell University Press, 1966.

Rediger, G. Lloyd. *Clergy Killers: Guidance for Pastors and Congregations Under Attack.* Louisville, KY: Westminster John Knox Press, 1997.

Scholey, Arthur. *The Discontented Dervishes: And Other Persian Tales Retold from Sádi by Arthur Scholey.* London: Watkins Publishing, 2002.

Schwartz, Howard, ed. *Tales of Wisdom: One Hundred Modern Parables.* New York: Crescent Books, 1995.

Shah, Idries. *Tales of the Dervishes: Teaching-Stories of the Sufi Masters over the Past Thousand Years.* Hertfordshire, UK: Granada Publishing Limited, 1973.

———. *The Way of the Sufi.* New York: E. P. Dutton & Co., Inc., 1970.

Simon, Uriel. "The Poor Man's Ewe-Lamb: An Example of a Juridical Parable." *Biblica* 48 (1967): 207–42.

Thoma, Clemens, and Michael Wyschogrod, eds. *Parable and Story in Judaism and Christianity.* Mahwah, NJ: Paulist Press, 1989.

Van Dyke, Henry. *Half-Told Tales.* New York: Charles Scribner's Sons, 1925.

Van Dyke, Henry, and Tertius Van Dyke. *Light My Candle: A Book of Reflections.* New York: Fleming H. Revell Company, 1926.

Via, Dan Otto, Jr. *The Parables: Their Literary and Existential Dimension.* Philadelphia, PA: Fortress Press, 1980 (1967).

Voris, Steven J. "Finding the Right Church." *Monday Morning: A Magazine for Presbyterian Leaders* 61, no. 18 (Nov. 4, 1996): 5.

———. "Parable of Hypocrisy." *The Priest* 53, no. 8 (August 1997): 6.

Watts, John D.W. *Isaiah 1—33.* Word Biblical Commentary. Vol. 24. Edited by David A. Hubbard et al. Waco, TX: Word Books, 1985.

Wayman, Alex, ed. *Buddhist Parables.* Buddhist Tradition Series. Vol. 13. Translated by Eugene Watson Burlingame. Delhi, India: Motilal Banarsidass Publishers Private Limited, 1999 (1922).

NOTES

Chapter One

1. *The Oyster and the Eagle: Selected Aphorisms and Parables of Multatuli,* ed. and trans. E. M. Beekman (Amherst, MA: University of Massachusetts Press, 1974), 52.

2. Lawrence Boadt, "Understanding the *Mashal* and Its Value for the Jewish-Christian Dialogue in a Narrative Theology," in *Parable and Story in Judaism and Christianity,* ed. Clemens Thoma and Michael Wyschogrod (Mahwah, NJ: Paulist Press, 1989), 174.

3. Joachim Jeremias, *The Parables of Jesus,* 2nd rev. ed. (New York: Charles Scribner's Sons, 1972), 20.

4. *Webster's New Collegiate Dictionary* (Springfield, MA: G & C Merriam Company, 1977), 830.

5. George Buttrick, *The Parables of Jesus* (New York: Harper & Brothers Publishers, 1928), xv.

6. Clarence Edward Macartney, *The Parables of the Old Testament* (New York: Fleming H. Revell Company, 1926), 8.

7. Henry Van Dyke and Tertius Van Dyke, *Light My Candle: A Book of Reflections* (New York: Fleming H. Revell Company, 1926), 272.

8. C. H. Dodd, *The Parables of the Kingdom,* rev. ed. (New York: Charles Scribner's Sons, 1961), 5.

9. Robert Funk quoted in Lawrence Boadt, "Understanding the *Mashal,*" 162.

10. Corbins Carnell and Madeleine Boucher, "Parable," in *A Dictionary of Biblical Tradition in English Literature,* ed. David Lyle Jeffrey (Grand Rapids, MI: Eerdmans, 1992), 582.

11. Andrew Greeley qtd. in Diarmuid O'Murchu, *Quantum Theology* (New York: The Crossroad Publishing Company, 1999), 93.

12. George Lakoff and Mark Johnson, *Metaphors We Live By* (Chicago, IL: The University of Chicago Press, 1980), 4.

13. Ibid., 5.

Chapter Two

1. John Dominic Crossan, *The Dark Interval: Towards a Theology of Story* (Niles, IL: Argus Communications, 1975), 87.

2. James W. Earl, "Prophecy and Parable in Medieval Apocalyptic History," *Religion and Literature* 31 (Spring 1999): 36.

3. *The Gospel of Buddha,* comp. Paul Carus (Middlesex, UK: Tiger Books International, 1995), 179.

4. Arnold J. Band, "The Bratslav Theory of the Sacred Tale," in *Nahman of Bratslav: The Tales,* trans. Arnold J. Band (Mahwah, NJ: Paulist Press, 1978), 34–36.

5. Clemens Thoma, "Literary and Theological Aspects of the Rabbinic Parables," in *Parable and Story in Judaism and Christianity,* ed. Clemens Thoma and Michael Wyschogrod (Mahwah, NJ: Paulist Press, 1989), 27.

6. Ibid., 28–30.

7. Idries Shah, *Tales of the Dervishes: Teaching-Stories of the Sufi Masters over the Past Thousand Years* (Hertfordshire, UK: Granada Publishing Limited, 1973), 38.

8. Idries Shah, *The Way of the Sufi* (New York: E. P. Dutton & Co., Inc., 1970), 197.

9. Shah, *Tales of the Dervishes,* 38.

Chapter Three

1. Majjhima i. 133–134 quoted in *Buddhist Parables,* Buddhist Tradition Series, Vol. 13, trans. Eugene Watson Burlingame, ed. Alex Wayman (Delhi, India: Motilal Banarsidass Publishers Private Limited, 1999), 185.

2. Shah, *Tales of the Dervishes,* 31.

3. Walter Nash, *The Language of Humour,* English Language Series Title No. 16 (New York: Longman Inc., 1985), 6.

Chapter Four

1. *The Lotus Sutra,* trans. Burton Watson (New York: Columbia University Press, 1993), 50.

2. Chris Baldrick, *The Concise Oxford Dictionary of Literary Terms* (Oxford and New York: Oxford University Press, 1990), 134.

3. Dan Otto Via, Jr., *The Parables: Their Literary and Existential Dimension* (Philadelphia, PA: Fortress Press, 1980), 7.

4. Ibid., 6.

5. Steven J. Voris, "Finding the Right Church," *Monday Morning: A Magazine for Presbyterian Leaders* 61, no. 18 (Nov. 4, 1996): 5.

6. Charles Schwartz, "Left Out," in *Tales of Wisdom: One Hundred Modern Parables,* ed. Howard Schwartz (New York: Crescent Books, 1995), 311.

7. Marvin Cohen, *The Monday Rhetoric of the Love Club and Other Parables* (New York: New Directions Publishing Corporation, 1973), 15–17.

8. *The Poetry of Robert Frost,* ed. Edward Connery Lathem (New York: Holt, Rinehart and Winston, 1969), 105.

Chapter Five

1. This fable appears on www.AesopFables.com.

2. Macartney, *The Parables of the Old Testament,* 10.

3. Barnabas Lindars, "Jotham's Fable: A New Form-Critical Analysis," *Journal of Theological Studies* 24 (October 1973): 361.

4. See www.aesopfables.com.

5. Roger J. Corless, *The Vision of Buddhism: The Space Under the Tree* (New York: Paragon House, 1989), 47.

6. *Jataka* 37:i.217–220 quoted in *Buddhist Parables,* 60–62.

7. Shah, *Tales of the Dervishes,* 76.

8. See www.aesopfables.com.

9. Enrique Anderson Imbert, *The Other Side of the Mirror,* trans. Isabel Reade (Carbondale, IL: Southern Illinois University Press, 1966), 3–5.

10. James Thurber, *The 13 Clocks* (New York: Dell Publishing, 1978).

Chapter Six

1. David C. Korten, *The Great Turning: From Empire to Earth Community* (San Francisco, CA: Berrett-Koehler Publishers, Inc., 2006), 310–11.

2. Augustine, *Sermon on the Mount, Harmony of the Gospels, Homilies on the Gospels,* Nicene and Post-Nicene Fathers, First Series, vol. 6, ed. Philip Schaff et al., trans. R. G. MacMullen (Peabody, MA: Hendrickson Publishers, Inc., 1994), 375.

3. John Calvin, *Commentary on a Harmony of the Evangelists, Matthew, Mark, and Luke,* vol. 2, trans. William Pringle (Grand Rapids, MI: Wm. B. Eerdmans Publishing Company, 1949), 410.

4. Ibid., 409.

5. Jeremias, *The Parables of Jesus,* 35–36.

6. *Meister Eckhart: The Essential Sermons, Commentaries, Treatises, and Defense,* The Classics of Western Spirituality: A Library of the Great Spiritual Masters (Mahwah, NJ: Paulist Press, 1981), 93.

7. Shah, *Tales of the Dervishes,* 20.

Chapter Seven

1. Anthony de Mello, *The Song of the Bird* (New York: Doubleday, 1984), 78.

2. Steven J. Voris, "Parable of Hypocrisy," *The Priest* 53, no. 8 (August 1997): 6.

3. Thomas Merton, *No Man Is an Island* (Garden City, NY: Doubleday & Company, Inc., 1967), 145.

4. Arthur Scholey, *The Discontented Dervishes: And Other Persian Tales Retold from Sádi by Arthur Scholey* (London: Watkins Publishing, 2002), 40–42.

5. Shah, *Tales of the Dervishes,* 141.

6. G. Lloyd Rediger, *Clergy Killers: Guidance for Pastors and Congregations Under Attack* (Louisville, KY: Westminster John Knox Press, 1997).

7. Shah, *Tales of the Dervishes,* 180.

8. Martin Goldsmith, "Parabolic Preaching in the Context of Islam," *Evangelical Review of Theology* 15 (July 1991): 272–77.

Chapter Eight

1. de Mello, *The Song of the Bird,* xvi.

2. Henry Van Dyke, *Half-Told Tales* (New York: Charles Scribner's Sons, 1925), viii.

3. Shah, *Tales of the Dervishes,* 20.

4. Otto Via, *The Parables: Their Literary and Existential Dimension,* 4.

5. Heinz Politzer, *Franz Kafka: Parable and Paradox,* rev. and expanded ed. (Ithaca, NY: Cornell University Press, 1966), 9–11.

Chapter Nine

1. Todd Outcalt, *Candles in the Dark: A Treasury of the World's Most Inspiring Parables* (Hoboken, NJ: John Wiley & Sons, Inc., 2002), 5.

2. Spencer Johnson, *Who Moved My Cheese?* (New York: G.P. Putnam's Sons, 1998).

3. Shah, *Tales of the Dervishes,* 50.

Chapter Ten

1. Outcalt, *Candles in the Dark*, 186.

Chapter Eleven

1. Bernard Brandon Scott, *Re-Imagine the World: An Introduction to the Parables of Jesus* (Santa Rosa, CA: Polebridge Press, 2001), 13–14.
2. David Buttrick, *Speaking Parables: A Homiletic Guide* (Louisville, KY: Westminster John Knox Press, 2000), 211.
3. William R. Herzog II, *Parables as Subversive Speech: Jesus as Pedagogue of the Oppressed* (Louisville, KY: Westminster/ John Knox Press, 1994), 233–58.
4. John Stanley Glen, qtd. in Herzog, 127.

Chapter Twelve

1. This fable appears on www.aesopfables.com.

ANNOTATED
BIBLIOGRAPHY

Literary Parables

These are parables that come out of literary circles instead of religious traditions.

Bartek, Edward J. *A Treasury of Parables.* New York: Philosophical Library, 1959.
The collection of seventy-nine philosophical parables, as a whole, seeks to unify all previous philosophical principles. Each parable is followed by three concluding proverbs.

Borges, Jorge Luis. *Labyrinths: Selected Stories and Other Writings.* Edited by Donald A. Yates and James E. Irby. Preface by Andre Maurois. New York: New Directions Publishing Corporation, 1964 (1962).
Eight parables are included in this collection of short experimental writings translated from the Spanish originals by this early twentieth-century Argentinian author.

Cohen, Marvin. *The Monday Rhetoric of the Love Club and Other Parables.* New York: New Directions Books, 1973.
A collection of twenty-one experimental short stories and parables.

Imbert, Enrique Anderson. *The Other Side of the Mirror.* Translated by Isabel Reade. Carbondale, IL: Southern Illinois University Press, 1966.
A collection of thirty-one short stories and parables by an

Argentinian American professor of Spanish literature. Originally written in Spanish, these stories blur the boundaries between reality and magic, life and death, dreaming and waking. The stories are often disturbing and leave the reader disoriented: a virtual gold mine for the interpreter of parables.

Johnson, Spencer. *Who Moved My Cheese?* New York: G. P. Putnam's Sons, 1998.
This parable is written primarily for businesspeople who are afraid to make changes. The book was also made into an animated video.

Kafka, Franz. *The Complete Stories and Parables.* Edited by Nahum N. Glatzer. New York: Quality Paperback Book Club, 1971.
This book, as well as many similar editions, contains thirty-two parables written by the early twentieth-century Austrian-Czech parabolic master. Look for clues to the interpretation of each parable in the title.

Multatuli. *The Oyster and the Eagle: Selected Aphorisms and Parables of Multatuli.* Edited and translated by E. M. Beekman. Amherst, MA: University of Massachusetts Press, 1974.
Multatuli is the pseudonym of Holland's greatest nineteenth-century novelist. The parables and proverbs from his literary works extracted for this collection are countercultural and frequently have social justice themes.

Poe, Edgar Allan. *The Works of Edgar Allan Poe in One Volume.* New York: Black's Readers Service Company, 1927.
This nineteenth-century American author is noted for being one of the earliest writers of horror. Several of his stories can be classified as parables, notably: "The Oval Portrait," "Shadow," and "Silence."

Prather, Hugh, and Gayle Prather. *Parables From Other Planets: Folktales of the Universe.* New York: Bantam Books, 1991.
A cleverly conceived collection of forty-two parables set on fic-

tional planets. The themes are relevant to problems on earth. The Prathers are late twentieth-century American therapists.

Schwartz, Howard, ed. *Tales of Wisdom: One Hundred Modern Parables.* New York: Crescent Books, 1995.
An excellent collection of the very best parables from the nineteenth and early to mid-twentieth centuries. Biographical notes about the authors in the appendix also list other works they have written. This is the single best work for getting started in reading parables.

Christian Parables

The Bible
Jesus's parables are found scattered throughout the first three books of the New Testament: Matthew, Mark, and Luke. There are between forty and sixty-four parables, depending on whether sentence metaphors are classified as parables and depending on whether duplicate parables found in more than one gospel are counted once, twice, or thrice. Large concentrations are found in Mark 4, Matthew 13, and Luke 15—16, 18.

De Mello, Anthony. *The Song of the Bird.* New York: Doubleday, 1984.
A collection of 123 parables from a variety of religious traditions adapted for Christians encouraging spiritual growth. De Mello was a Roman Catholic priest from India who died in 1992.

Hays, Edward. *The Ethiopian Tattoo Shop.* Easton, KS: Forest of Peace Books, Inc., 1983.
A collection of twenty-two parables neatly linked together under the guise of a Christian tattooist using the stories as a painkiller. Hints for interpretation are included in an appendix.

Kierkegaard, Søren. *Parables of Kierkegaard.* Edited by Thomas C. Oden. Princeton, NJ: Princeton University Press, 1989 (1978).
This collection of eighty-six parables extracted from this nineteenth-century Danish Christian's philosophical writings are

mostly teaching-metaphor parables that originally served to illustrate abstract points.

Outcalt, Todd. *Candles in the Dark: A Treasury of the World's Most Inspiring Parables.* Hoboken, NJ: John Wiley & Sons, Inc., 2002.
A collection of modernized parables from a variety of religious traditions put together by an American United Methodist minister.

Singh, Sundar. *Wisdom of the Sadhu: Teachings of Sundar Singh.* Compiled and edited by Kim Comer. Farmington, PA: Plough Publishing House, 2000.
Nearly thirty parables throughout the work (not all are labeled as such) help the seeker draw closer to God. Singh was an early twentieth-century Indian Christian who converted from Sikhism and refused to accept the Western forms of denominational Christianity.

Van De Weyer, Robert. *Celtic Parables.* Nashville, TN: Abingdon Press, 1999.
A collection of brief stories about the Christian missionary activities of fourteen Celtic saints. The stories are not so much parables in the true sense, but brief miracle stories that can be entertaining, inspirational, and/or transformative.

Van Dyke, Henry. *Half-Told Tales.* New York: Charles Scribner's Sons, 1925.
Intriguing parables primarily in the *unfinished tale style* leave readers to imagine what happens next. Van Dyke was an early twentieth-century American Presbyterian minister and professor of English Literature at Princeton University.

Jewish Parables

Band, Arnold J., trans. *Nahman of Bratslav: The Tales.* Introduction and commentaries also by Arnold J. Band. The

Classics of Western Spirituality Series. Mahwah, NJ: Paulist Press, 1978.
Thirteen parabolic stories by this early nineteenth-century Jewish master appear in this book. Interpretations of each tale follow in an appendix with commentary format.

Bleefeld, Rabbi Bradley N., and Robert L. Shook, eds. *Saving the World Entire and 100 Other Beloved Parables from the Talmud.* New York: Penguin Putnam Inc., 1998.
As the title suggests, this is a collection of 101 parables from the Talmud. Each parable is followed by a "Rabbi's Comment" that explains the parable's meaning.

Bronstein, Rabbi Yisrael, ed. *Jewish Parables: A Mashal for Every Occasion.* Adapted by Rabbi Moshe Gelbein from the Hebrew. Brooklyn, NY: Mesorah Publications, Ltd., 2004.
Each of the 267 parables from the Jewish tradition in this collection is concluded with a brief exhortation.

Buber, Martin. *Tales of the Hasidim: The Early Masters.* New York: Schocken Books, 1972 (1947).
This book contains dozens of parables scattered throughout a collection of miracle stories, proverbs, and teachings of the Hasidic masters. Buber is credited with popularizing the teachings of the Hasidic masters for twentieth-century audiences. He is dinged by critics for taking liberties with some of his translations.

Muslim Parables

The Qur'ān
There are several parables scattered throughout Islam's holy book. Concentrations of parables can be found in Surahs 13–16, 18, 22, 24–29, 36, and 39.

Scholey, Arthur. *The Discontented Dervishes: And Other Persian Tales Retold from Sādi by Arthur Scholey.* London: Watkins Publishing, 2002.

A collection of seventy-four short stories and parables from the thirteenth-century Sufi teacher Sádi.

Shah, Idries. *Tales of the Dervishes: Teaching-Stories of the Sufi Masters over the Past Thousand Years.* Hertfordshire, UK: Granada Publishing Limited, 1973 (1967).
This is a collection of eighty-two parables from diverse Muslim sources spanning 1,400 years. Each parable is followed by a brief explanation and biographical note on the supposed author.

Eastern Parables

Buddhist Parables. Buddhist Tradition Series. Vol. 13. Translated by Eugene Watson Burlingame. Edited by Alex Wayman. Delhi, India: Motilal Banarsidass Publishers Private Limited, 1999 (1922).
This is a collection of over two hundred parables and *jataka* extracted from Buddhist teachings through the centuries. A scholarly introduction and careful bibliographic citations for each parable allow the reader to find the original source and context for each parable.

Das, Surya. *The Snow Lion's Turquoise Mane: Wisdom Tales From Tibet.* New York: HarperSanFrancisco, 1992.
This is a collection of 150 wisdom tales and parables from the Tibetan Buddhist tradition.

Lim, Joyce, trans. *100 Parables of Zen.* Illustrated by N. S. Chen. Singapore: Asiapac Books PTE LTD, 1995.
Ninety-eight brief parabolic stories collected together in the fifth century. The stories are presented in comic book format and each story is concluded with a proverb.

The Lotus Sutra. Translated by Burton Watson. New York: Columbia University Press, 1993.
Ancient parable-filled text in the Buddhist tradition.

Fables

Aesop's Fables
Hundreds of editions of Aesop's fables have been issued through the centuries. Some 655 fables have been attributed to this sixth-century BCE fabulist. No collection or study of fables can be complete without Aesop.

Beichner, Paul E. *Once Upon a Parable: Fables for the Present.* Notre Dame, IN: The University of Notre Dame Press, 1974. This is a collection of eighty fables. Three quarters are written by Paul Beichner, who taught medieval studies at the University of Notre Dame, and the remaining quarter are adapted from Odo of Cheriton (circa 1247). The collection does not distinguish authorship of individual fables. A moral is attached to each fable.

Selected Fables & Tales of La Fontaine. A Signet Classic. Translated by Marie Ponsot. New York: The New American Library, 1966.
This book offers more than ninety fables from the seventeenth-century French fabulist Jean de la Fontaine. Many different editions of his works are available.

Stories from The Thousand and One Nights. The Harvard Classics. Edited by Charles W. Eliot. Translated by Edward William Lane. Revised by Stanley Lane-Poole. New York: P. F. Collier & Son Corporation, 1969 (1909).
Though technically a collection of short stories connected by a bedtime-story theme, some of the stories have an implied moral and drift into the world of parable and fable.

Tales of the Brothers Grimm. Edited by Clarissa Pinkola Estes. New York: Quality Paperback Book Club, 1999.
Some fifty-three ancient folk stories or fairy tales by the nineteenth-century German brothers, Jakob and Wilhelm Grimm, are in this book.

INDEX OF PARABLES

INDEX OF PARABLES TO THE ROMAN CATHOLIC AND THE REVISED COMMON LECTIONARIES

Fig Tree (Luke 13:6–9), pp. 187–92
 Roman Catholic: Third Sunday of Lent, Year C
 Roman Catholic: Saturday of the 29th Week of the Year,
  Years 1 & 2
 Revised Common: Lent 3, Year C

Good Samaritan (Luke 10:25–37), pp. 45–47
 Roman Catholic: Fifteenth Sunday of the Year, Year C
 Roman Catholic: Monday of the 27th Week of the Year,
  Years 1 & 2
 Revised Common: Proper 10, Year C, Sunday   ·
 Revised Common: Easter 5, Year C, Wednesday
 Revised Common: Proper 26, Year B, Saturday

Isaiah's Vision and Call (Isa 6:1–8), pp. 26–28
 Roman Catholic: Fifth Sunday of the Year, Year C
 Roman Catholic: Saturday of the 14th Week of the Year,
  Year 2
 Revised Common: Trinity Sunday, Year B, Sunday
 Revised Common: Easter 3, Year C, Wednesday
 Revised Common: Epiphany 5, Year C, Sunday
 Revised Common: Easter 3, Year C, Friday
 Revised Common: January 4, Year C

Isaiah's Vision Concerning God's People (Isa 5:18–23), pp. 28
 Roman Catholic: none
 Revised Common: Trinity Sunday, Year B, Saturday
 Revised Common: Proper 15, Year C, Monday
 Revised Common: Proper 20, Year C, Saturday

Jairus's Daughter (Mark 5:21–43), p. 170
 Roman Catholic: Thirteenth Sunday of the Year, Year B
 Roman Catholic: Tuesday of the 4th Week of the Year,
  Years 1 & 2
 Revised Common: Proper 8, Year B, Sunday

Jotham's Fable (Judg 9:8–15), pp. 87–88
 Roman Catholic: Wednesday of the 20th Week of the Year,
  Year 1

Revised Common: Lent 3, Year C, Wednesday
Revised Common: Proper 12, Year A, Wednesday
Revised Common: Easter 5, Year B, Saturday

Nebuchadnezzar's Dream (Dan 4:10–12), pp. 187–92
  Roman Catholic: none
  Revised Common: Proper 28, Year B, Thursday

Pharisee and the Tax Collector (Luke 18:10–14), p. 124
  Roman Catholic: Thirtieth Sunday of the Year, Year C
  Roman Catholic: Saturday of the 3rd Week in Lent,
    Years 1 & 2
  Revised Common: Proper 25, Year C, Sunday

Pounds, the (Luke 19:12–27); "talents"
  (Matt 25:14–30), pp. 101–3
  Roman Catholic: Wednesday of the 33rd Week of the Year,
    Years 1 & 2
  Revised Common: Proper 26, Year C, Wednesday
  Revised Common: Proper 28, Year A, Sunday

Prodigal Son (Luke 15:11–32), p. 186
  Roman Catholic: Fourth Sunday of Lent, Year C
  Roman Catholic: Saturday of the 2nd Week of Lent
  Revised Common: Lent 4, Year C, Sunday

Purpose of Parable (Matt 13:10–17), pp. 25–26
  Roman Catholic: Thursday of the 16th Week of the Year,
    Years 1 & 2
  Revised Common: Proper 10, Year A, Wednesday

Rich Man and Lazarus (Luke 16:19–31), pp. 181–86
  Roman Catholic: Twenty-sixth Sunday of the Year,
    Year C
  Roman Catholic: Thursday of the 2nd Week of Lent,
    Years 1 & 2
  Revised Common: Proper 21, Year C, Sunday
  Revised Common: Proper 23, Year B, Wednesday

Rich Young Ruler (Matt 19:16–22), p. 122
    Roman Catholic: Monday of the 20th Week of the Year,
      Years 1 & 2
    Revised Common: Proper 25, Year A, Wednesday
    Revised Common: Proper 21, Year C, Wednesday

Righteous Society (Isa 32:1–8), pp. 26–29
    Roman Catholic: none
    Revised Common: Proper 18, Year B, Friday

Stone That the Builders Rejected (Ps 118:22–23), pp. 120–21
    Roman Catholic: Easter, the Resurrection of the Lord,
      Easter Vigil, Years A, B & C
    Roman Catholic: Easter Sunday, Years A, B & C
    Roman Catholic: Second Sunday of Easter, Years A, B & C
    Roman Catholic: Fourth Sunday of Easter, Year B
    Revised Common: Easter, Years A, B & C; Sunday,
      Monday, Tuesday, Wednesday
    Revised Common: Passion/Palm Sunday, Years A, B & C,
      Sunday
    Revised Common: Passion/Palm Sunday, Year B; Thursday,
      Friday, Saturday
    Revised Common: Easter 2, Year C, Sunday
    Revised Common: Lent 2, Year C, Saturday

Tear Out Own Eye (Matt 5:29), p. 171
    Roman Catholic: Friday of the 10th Week of the Year,
      Years 1 & 2
    Revised Common: Epiphany 6, Year A, Sunday
    Revised Common: Proper 22, Year B, Wednesday

Ten Maidens (Matt 25:1–13), p. 174
    Roman Catholic: Thirty-second Sunday of the Year,
      Year A
    Roman Catholic: Friday of the 21st Week of the Year,
      Years 1 & 2
    Revised Common: Proper 27, Year A, Sunday
    Revised Common: Epiphany 2, Year B, Saturday

Test of Pleasure (Eccl 2:1–11), pp. 163–67
  Roman Catholic: none
  Revised Common: Baptism of the Lord, Year C, Friday

Two Sons (Matt 21:23–32), pp. 30–31
  Roman Catholic: Twenty-sixth Sunday of the Year, Year A
  Roman Catholic: Monday of the 3rd Week in Advent,
    Years 1 & 2
  Roman Catholic: Tuesday of the 3rd Week in Advent,
    Year 1 & 2
  Revised Common: Proper 21, Year A, Sunday
  Revised Common: Proper 19, Year B, Saturday
  Revised Common: Proper 25, Year C, Wednesday
  Revised Common: Advent 3, Year B, Saturday

Wealth (Eccl 5:8–20), pp. 163–67
  Roman Catholic: none
  Revised Common: Proper 20, Year B, Wednesday

Wheat and Tares (Matt 13:24–30), p. 23
  Roman Catholic: Sixteenth Sunday of the Year, Year A
  Roman Catholic: Saturday of the 16th Week of the Year,
    Years 1 & 2
  Revised Common: Proper 11, Year A, Sunday

Wicked Tenants (Matt 21:33–46; Mark 12:1–2; Luke 20:9–19),
    pp. 119–21
  Roman Catholic: Friday of the 2nd Week of Lent,
    Years 1 & 2
  Revised Common: Proper 22, Year A, Saturday
  Revised Common: Proper 28, Year B, Saturday